CHANGING
THE WORLD
PRESS

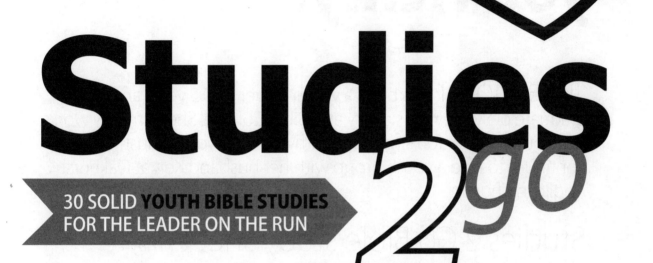

Studies 2go

**30 SOLID YOUTH BIBLE STUDIES
FOR THE LEADER ON THE RUN**

Julie Moser

'Let the word of Christ dwell in you richly.'

Julie Moser has been a youth leader for 15 years and is a graduate of Sydney Missionary and Bible College. She currently works as a youth advisor for Anglican Youthworks in Sydney, Australia, and continues to lead a youth group with her husband Ken at Oakhurst Anglican Church.

Special thanks to Christine Kotsaris.

Dedicated to the volunteer, part-time and full-time youth leaders in the Western region of Sydney and Bishop Brian King for his loving support of their ministry.

Published August 2002
Copyright 2002 Julie Moser

Design and illustration Anthony Wallace
Editor Michelle Haines Thomas

Table of contents

Introduction

Bible studies

Yr 2 (Back to Basics) Supplement with Growing More like Jesus.

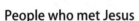

Yr 3 Autum Term.

Yr 5. Spring Term.

Yr 4 Spring Term.

Hey, this is easy.

The fact that you have this book means you are either running or are about to run a small group Bible study for youth.

If you are like most of us and time is limited this book will provide you with instant photocopiable studies that you can use with a minimum of preparation. To be honest I don't even stop to read these kinds of introductions but just go straight to the material. However, the following information will help you to know how to use these studies more effectively with tips on how to run a small group. So please read on...

Running a small group bible study

Who?

These studies are designed to be used in weekly small group Bible studies for high school age youth. For a variety of reasons it is most desirable that Bible study groups for young people are single sex. A single sex group will allow them to participate in the study more easily and therefore learn more, and application can be more specific. It is more appropriate to have mature Christian men discipling young men and mature Christian women discipling young girls, which is done more effectively in single sex groups. Finally, maturity levels are very different between girls and guys during the high school years and combining them will make your job more difficult.

Time

Set a time for your group to meet. A good length of time for youth is about 90 minutes as it gives you time to talk, eat, and have a study. Choose a time that is best for everyone, keeping it not too late for a younger group. Try to keep it exactly the same time and same day every week so that it becomes a routine that is not forgotten.

Place

The ideal is that the group is hosted at the leader's home. This deepens the relationship with the leader/s and gives them the opportunity to show hospitality. When this is not possible you could:

Ask someone in your church with the gift of hospitality to host your group.

Meet in the home of one of the young people whose parents are sympathetic.

Meet at the church property.

Try to keep the same location each week as a different venue requires some adjusting and can make it harder for the young people to be settled for the study.

An important note: It is important to take child protection issues into account when involved with young people. With any venue you use, especially your own home, you need to consider protocol guidelines that ensure that you are not alone with a child. You need to consider situations where only one child may turn up or one child may turn up early or leave late. There are things that you can do that will ensure both safety for the child and your reputation. For example, work with a co-leader or have your study when your husband/wife/housemates/parents are home.

Leaders need a set of guidelines, endorsed by the pastor/elders of the church, that are understood and to which they adhere.

A helpful course is: **'Child Protection Essentials'**

Available through: **Anglican Youthworks**

PO Box A287,

Sydney South 1235

Australia

Telephone: 02 8268 3388

or Email: info@youthworks.asn.au

Give your group an identity

Do things together outside the regular meeting time. This will develop deeper friendships within the group and with you, the leader. It also makes your group something special that will give the young people a sense of belonging. Some suggestions of socials/special events are: have a pizza dinner together; go to a movie; hold a sleepover at the church or one of their houses; go to the beach or local pool; do a service project for the church; take some suggestions from the group of the things they would like to do.

Using the Bible

Never assume that your young people know anything about the Bible, including what the big numbers (chapters) and little numbers (verses) are, or terms such as Old Testament and New Testament. Teach all of this from the very beginning. A helpful way to start a Bible study could be to use 'The Bible' study sheet on page 9. Have Bibles available for the young people to use but encourage them to use their own. If they do not have one, or they do not have one with modern English, then talk to them or their parents about which one is the best for them, or buy it for them.

Using these Bible studies

One-year plan

These 30 studies should last you a year. Although there are 52 weeks in the year, most groups don't meet during the summer break and have weeks throughout the year where Bible study makes way for camps, socials etc. You will probably find that there will be weeks when you want to present a study that you have written dealing with specific issues facing your group. A one-year plan prevents you from being directionless in the material you cover, and also makes sure you don't double up on studies or neglect important topics.

You can use these studies in any order you wish. It is suggested, however, that you cover 'What is a Christian' first so that your group knows the basics of what a Christian believes, and then 'The Bible' to prepare them for using the Bible throughout the year.

The study

Modifications
Not every study is suitable for every group. You may find there are questions or sections you want to delete or modify.

Time
Each study is designed to take up to 45 minutes (except for the end-of-year 'Christmas' study). If you finish early you can use the remaining time for a longer prayer time, or just use the time chatting and relating. If you don't complete the study, don't panic. You can always finish it off the following week. Your goal is not to get through the study. Your goal is for your group to learn and enjoy learning. So if a study takes two weeks, or even three, and it is a productive time, don't cut it short simply to complete the sheet. Similarly you may find you do not finish the study but that you have covered the material you want to and so can move on to another one the following week.

Golden rule: You are not a slave to the study!

Leaders' notes

These notes are to help you in preparation. You will need to have a copy of the Bible study handout with you as you go through the leaders' notes, so that you can write in answers and make comments if you need to. The leaders' notes are for preparation only and not designed for you to use during the Bible study, so make sure you read them ahead of time.

Use these Bible studies as a model

Over time, as you get used to running a small group Bible study, you may find you have the confidence to write your own studies. These studies are a model of a format you can adopt to write your own. They are not the only format and you will develop your own style. You can also draw on the material in these studies to write your own. Take the parts you need, and discard the parts you don't need, and modify them to suit your group.

A helpful pattern to get you started to write your own studies is:

1. Sharing question.

2. An exercise to introduce the subject (see some examples in the studies in this book).

3. Read the passage/s.

4. Ask some questions that will help them think through what the passage is teaching.

5. Apply what they have learned to their own context.

6. Pray.

Discussion starters/sharing questions

Each study will begin with a discussion starter in the form of questions, a quiz or an activity. Discussion starters prepare your group for the topic and help you to work out what each person thinks, believes or doubts about the subject. Don't be afraid to spend a bit of time in this section if it is a healthy, focussed discussion. This can often become a constructive 'question and answer' time.

Sharing questions are also a helpful tool in teaching young people to contribute and to listen to each other. The loud, talkative person learns to listen to others and the shy, quiet person learns to contribute and have the experience of people listening when they speak. The quiet person will also be more inclined to contribute later during the study once they have already had a postive experience of sharing an answer. It is important to keep control of a sharing time. In order for it to be a worthwhile exercise, make sure that others listen while someone is sharing.

Questions are designed to be simple, fun and thought-provoking. Each question is simple enough that you can insist on people giving an answer. Don't accept an "I don't know" answer, but offer to come back to them once others have answered. You may wish to ask the sharing questions before handing out the sheet in order for the questions to be a surprise to the group. If your group is not confident, they may feel more comfortable with the questions right in front of them from the beginning.

Feel free to add your own discussion starter at the beginning of the study in addition to the ones already on the sheet. A helpful question to start off every study is: Rate your week from 1-10 (1 is terrible and 10 is fantastic).

Warning: Beware of unhelpful distractions and going around in circles in your discussion time. Remember that your Bible study exists to, among other things, study the Bible!

Answering questions

You will face many questions that you may not feel confident to answer. Don't be concerned if you don't know all the answers. Try your best to answer a question if you have something to say about it. However, a satisfactory answer is sometimes: "I'll look into it and get back to you next week". Preparing your topic with plenty of time beforehand will give you the opportunity to do some research. As well as regular personal Bible reading, reading Christian books is a great way of improving your biblical knowledge.

Some reading suggestions are:

'Know The Truth'	by Bruce Milne (IVP)
'Know What You Believe'	by Paul Little (Victor)
'Gospel and Kingdom'	by Graeme Goldsworthy (Lancer)
'Ultimate Questions'	by John Blanchard (Evangelical Press)
'Know Why You Believe'	by Paul Little (Victor)

Prayer

Prayer is an important part of small group life and it must be a regular feature of the group. It is helpful to pray at the beginning of the study, perhaps immediately after the sharing questions, to help them focus on what they are about to study. At the end of each study there should be time for prayer. During this time you should ask for things to pray for in response to the study, as well as taking requests from individuals about personal needs. Don't forget to say prayers of thanks as well as making requests.

It is not necessary for everyone to share something to pray for, nor is it necessary for everyone to be involved in praying.

There are several ways you can pray. Here are a few:

Pray as a large group. It is helpful for someone to be nominated to start and someone, perhaps a leader, to finish.

You could break into pairs or triplets to share and pray. This requires the group to be a little more developed in their confidence to share and pray together.

Pray around the circle for the person next to you. You will need to offer the option of not praying by either tapping the person next to them, or by saying "pass".

You could have a time of silence for everyone to pray and then the leader concludes. It is better for the group to pray aloud, but this option is helpful when you have challenged them personally about something in the study, or the group is not yet confident to pray aloud, or if you don't have much time left for prayer.

Each person could pray by saying nothing more than, "Thank you Lord for _____ ."

Some groups like to keep a book of prayer points that can be revised over time to see how God answered prayers.

Be prepared that prayer in the early days of your group may not work too well - it can sometimes take months! It is something, however, that you must teach your group to do, and therefore you must persevere. It is up to you to teach your group both how to pray and why we pray. Requesting that eyes are closed is helpful to prevent distractions and also helps those who are not so confident to pray when they know others are not looking at them. Don't allow young people to misbehave, whisper to each other, pass notes or generally treat prayer with contempt. Your goal is that the group is a prayerful group, and that prayer also becomes a part of their daily routine.

Reading

Allocate Bible passages ahead of time so that searching for verses is done all at one time. Once you have a volunteer to read, write their name on your sheet so that you know who to call on when that verse needs to be read. If a passage is a particularly long one, divide it into paragraphs or a few verses for each person.

Some groups have young people who have English as a second language or who are illiterate and therefore not confident or capable of reading. It is important, therefore, not to put people on the spot and so embarrass them. Initially ask for volunteers, and over the first month or so note those who will not read. Sometimes it is a confidence problem and sometimes it is a reading difficulty. Don't be satisfied that a young person cannot read. The Christian faith is based on a person (Jesus) who is recorded in a book (the Bible). For you to help a young person develop in their faith you need to equip them to understand the Bible and you cannot do this effectively if they are never able to read it. You may need to find a way to help them to read. My experience has been that every young person who cannot read desperately wants to be able to. So once you know of someone who has difficulties, work out a plan to help them. It is helpful to say several times in the group something like:

"If you are not a confident reader, this group is the safest place for you to try to read because no-one here will laugh at you or make it difficult for you. I promise I will never force anyone to read out aloud, so if you want to have a try then just volunteer or ask for a short, easy verse."

One last thing...

Be prepared that when you run a youth Bible study, you will have 'successful' days and 'not so successful' days. Don't give up and don't think you are a failure when it is not so successful. Often running a Bible study requires patience and perseverance. Have a three year goal to develop them into mature young people. Sometimes we don't see the fruit of our labour in the first year! Pray for God's blessing and do your best.

If I can be a help at all in regards to the information in this book email me at kjmoser@hotmail.com and title the subject 'Bible Studies'.

Regards
Julie Moser

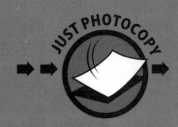

Leader's notes
What is a Christian?

Aim (By the end of the study the group members will know what a Christian believes and be challenged to think about what they believe.

Share Ask everyone to answer the sharing question. Their answers may give you some insight into what they believe. Accept both thoughtful and trivial answers.

What do you think MAKES someone a Christian? Here are the answers

a) Being baptised in a church.   T/**F**
b) Doing good things.   T/**F**
c) Trusting is Jesus.   **T**/F
d) Believing that God exists.   T/**F**
e) Helping others.   T/**F**
f) Going to church as much as possible.   T/**F**
g) Reading the Bible every day.   T/**F**
h) Eating healthy food.   T/**F**

Ask the young people to share their answers and be prepared to discuss briefly questions that may not be covered in this study. Some helpful Bible verses for you to know as you answer are: Ephesians 2:8-9 and James 2:19. You may need to make the distinction between what MAKES someone a Christian and what a Christian does BECAUSE they are a Christian.

What does a Christian believe?

Allocate people to read the following passages. After they read each passage ask for volunteers to explain what it says a Christian believes.

1 Corinthians 15:1-5 You are saved by the gospel, which is Jesus' death and resurrection for our sin.
1 Peter 3:18 Jesus, who was righteous, died for us who are unrighteous, to bring us to God.
Romans 6:23 Sin leads to death but Jesus brings eternal life.
1 John 1:8-9 We are all sinful, but if we confess our sin we are forgiven.
Romans 10:9 If we confess Jesus is Lord (outward sign) and believe it in our heart (inward sign) we will be saved.
1 John 4:15 If we acknowledge that Jesus is God's son, God lives in us.
1 John 2:3-6 A Christian is someone who obeys Jesus.

Ask for volunteers to complete the two statements about what is clear and unclear to them regarding what a Christian believes.
From the Bible passages above answer: **How does a person become a Christian?** Ask the group to reflect on the passages above and come up with an answer as to how someone becomes a Christian. The important issues are what God has done through Jesus, what a person believes about what God has done and how they express that belief.

What do I believe?

What are some hesitations people have about becoming a Christian? Ask for volunteers to give opinions about the hesitations people have and as they do ask everyone to write down all answers. Once you have a list ask them to circle the hesitations they also have and then ask for volunteers to share their answers.

Ask the group to tick the statements that are true for them and then discuss their answers.

Further reading Encourage them to think about reading the Gospel of John.

Pray Share matters for prayer and pray together.

What is a Christian?

Share
If you could ask God any question, what would you ask him?

What do you think MAKES someone a Christian?
Try this quick quiz:

a) Being baptised in a church.   T/F
b) Doing good things.   T/F
c) Trusting in Jesus.   T/F
d) Believing that God exists.   T/F
e) Helping others.   T/F
f) Going to church as much as possible.   T/F
g) Reading the Bible every day.   T/F
h) Eating healthy food.   T/F

Discuss your answers.

What does a Christian believe?

A Christian follows the teachings in the Bible. Below are some passages that outline the basic teachings of the Bible. **What do the following passages tell us about what a Christian believes?**

1 Corinthians 15:1-5

1 Peter 3:18

Romans 6:23

1 John 1:8-9

Romans 10:9

1 John 4:15

1 John 2:3-6

✔ One thing that is clear to me about what a Christian believes is

✘ One thing that is NOT clear to me about what a Christian believes is

From the Bible passages above answer:
How does a person become a Christian?

What do I believe?

What are some hesitations people have about becoming a Christian?
As you share your answers make a list below.

Circle any hesitations on the list that you might also share with others.

Tick below the statements that are true for you:

❏ I believe Jesus is the Son of God.
❏ I believe Jesus rose from the dead.
❏ I believe I am forgiven for my sin.
❏ I am certain I will go to heaven.
❏ I tell others I believe in Jesus.
❏ I believe the Bible tells me the truth about Jesus.
❏ I follow Jesus every day.
❏ People know I am a Christian.

Discuss your answers.

Further reading

The Gospel of John was written so that we might believe in Jesus and have eternal life (John 20:30-31). Think about reading the Gospel of John over the coming weeks.

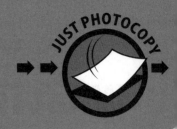

Leader's notes
The Bible

Aim (This study is to introduce the young people to the Bible and show them that it is God's word that contains the truth. It is also meant to challenge the young people about their personal Bible reading.

You may find some of the information in this study pretty basic for your group. It is important, however, that you make sure everyone is confident in even the most basic things, such as looking up a verse or knowing which books are in the Old Testament or the New Testament.

Share The best book (ie novel) they have ever read. For those who are not great readers, include answers such as comic books. Ask people to talk about common views about the Bible.

Introduction to the basics of the Bible

Read out the information about the Bible. Make sure everyone has understood what you have read. Then have a test run and ask the group to look up some places in the Bible: eg John 3:16, Leviticus 19:1. Sometimes you can be surprised at what you learn about your group in this exercise.

The Bible is made up of two sections - what are they? Old Testament and New Testament.

Naming books in the Old and New Testaments is not incredibly difficult for some. Be prepared, however, that there may be some young people in your group who know very little about the Bible. This exercise is to give them the opportunity to perhaps answer some questions correctly, and feel more confident that they know something. If this exercise is too easy for your young people, you can make it more of a challenge by asking them to name books starting with a certain letter, eg name all the OT books starting with the letter 'E'.

What the Bible is not: Read out this sentence and answer any questions regarding these false descriptions of the Bible. The passages below in the section 'What the Bible is' should help dispel any misconceptions about the Bible.

What the Bible is: Read out the statements and accompanying verses. Allow for possible questions.

To sum the Bible up in one sentence: Answer any questions they may have and consider memorising the statement.

What are some questions you have about the Bible? This is an opportunity for the young people to ask anything they like about the Bible.

Why do you think it is important to read the Bible? Some of the reasons will be clear from what has been read in the above verses.

What are some things which prevent you from reading the Bible? Suggest ways to overcome these.

Some ideas for reading the Bible

Read through each section here and perhaps set a plan for your whole group (eg memory verses, learning the books of the Bible etc). This section gives you the opportunity to speak to the group about what they already do or don't do regarding personal Bible reading, and to guide them to make plans that can improve what they already do. Help each person set plans for personal Bible reading. Each person may need to have different plans depending on the level of their spiritual maturity. Don't be too ambitious in your goals (eg Bible reading twice a day an hour each time). Start small and build from there. Suggest a time for prayer (make a prayer list?) and a plan for Bible reading (eg choose a book and read a chapter a day). Also encourage them to do it regularly (two or three times a week, or every school day, or even daily) and avoid any distractions where possible. In future weeks you might have a regular sharing time in your group about what they have read during the week.

Pray Share some matters for prayer and then pray.

The Bible

Half Time:

Share

What is the best book you have ever read? Why?

What do people say about the Bible?

What are some reasons people give for not reading the Bible?

Song:

Introduction to the basics of the Bible

The Bible is made up of 66 books written by different people. Each book is divided into chapters (the big number) and verses (the small number). To find a place in the Bible, the index is the first place to go. In time, it is helpful to start learning where all the books are located.

1 **The Bible is made up of two sections - what are they?**

2 **Can you name some books in the Old Testament?**

3 **Can you name some stories in the Old Testament?**

4 **Can you name some books in the New Testament?**

5 **Can you name some stories in the New Testament?**

What the Bible is not:

fairy tales, myths, a 'magic book' or an old, out-of-date history book.

What the Bible is:

Written to real people in real situations:
Luke 1:1-4
A guide on the way God wants you to live:
2 Timothy 3:14-17
Powerful and alive: **Hebrews 4:12-13**
The words of God: **2 Peter 1:20-21**

1 Tim 1:15
John 3:16

And God's Word becomes a person!
John 1:1-2 and 14 (see also Hebrews 1:1-3)
We cannot separate God's word from the person of Jesus. Jesus is the full expression of God's word. He spoke God's word and he **IS** God's word in the flesh.

To sum up the Bible up in one sentence:

The story of God's plan to destroy sin and death and bring salvation to his people.
God achieved his plan by sending his son Jesus to die on the cross to pay the penalty for our sin.

What are some questions you have about the Bible?

Why do you think it is important to read the Bible?

What are some things which prevent you from reading the Bible?
(Suggest ways to overcome these problems)

July Aug

Some ideas for reading the Bible

READ: Try reading the Bible on your own - you could start with one of the Gospels: Matthew, Mark, Luke or John. They all contain the story of Jesus. Write down questions you might have as you read.

PLAN AHEAD: Have a plan - share and discuss ways in which you can read the Bible more effectively, and write down a plan for what you can do this week.

MEMORISE: Try to memorise Bible verses - you could try to learn a new one every month. Try to memorise the Bible in one sentence (above). Try also to learn the books of the Bible in order - start with the New Testament books and then the Old Testament.

Prayer

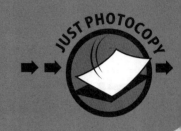

Aim (At the end of the study the group should understand what prayer is and what it takes to pray.

Share The two sharing questions introduce the idea of prayer as talking to God.

Tick the boxes: have the young people tick the box that best describes them and discuss their answers.

What are some things you find hard to understand about prayer? Spend a little time discussing the things they find difficult.

Read the following verses and write next to each one something it says to us about prayer. Allocate passages to readers before you start. This saves time looking up the passages. Be prepared to answer any questions that may come out of these passages.

Matthew 6:5-8	Don't do it to look good. Be genuine in your prayer.
Matthew 5:44	Pray for your enemies.
Ephesians 6:18	Pray always about anything.
Philippians 4:6	Pray when you are anxious about something.
1 Thessalonians 5:17	Do it regularly.

How does someone pray?

Have a volunteer read Matthew 6:9-13.

Write down some things Jesus tells us to pray:
Verse 9: Address God as 'Father' and praise his name.
10: That God's will be done.
11: Provision of what we need.
12: Forgiveness for us and help to forgive others.
13: Protection from temptation and the evil one.

What are some things in the Lord's prayer that you find easy to pray? (eg give us what we need)

What are some things in the Lord's prayer that you find difficult to pray? (eg forgive others)

Explain a simple pattern for prayer. This is a summary of the Lord's Prayer:
Give thanks to God for who he is and what he has done.
Pray for the needs of others.
Pray for your needs.

Putting it into practice!

Pray Share some concerns you have and pray for them in the group.

Think About meeting regularly with one or two other people to pray together.

Think About writing down your prayer requests in a book so you can remember what to pray for, and also see how God answers each prayer over time.

Individual studies

Prayer

Share

Who is someone you find easy to talk to? Why?

When is it hard to talk to someone?

Prayer is simply 'talking to God'. Put a tick in the box that best describes you and discuss your answers:

I find it easy to pray.
❏ Always ❏ Mostly ❏ Sometimes ❏ Never

I know what to pray for.
❏ Always ❏ Mostly ❏ Sometimes ❏ Never

I remember to pray every day.
❏ Always ❏ Mostly ❏ Sometimes ❏ Never

I feel comfortable praying out loud.
❏ Always ❏ Mostly ❏ Sometimes ❏ Never

I pray with other people.
❏ Always ❏ Mostly ❏ Sometimes ❏ Never

What are some things you find hard to understand about prayer?

Read the following verses and write next to each one something it says to us about prayer:

Matthew 6:5-8

Matthew 5:44

Ephesians 6:18

Philippians 4:6

1 Thessalonians 5:17

How does someone pray?

Jesus has given us a model of how we should pray. This model is called the 'Lord's Prayer'.

Read: Matthew 6:9-13

Write down some things Jesus tells us to pray:

Verse 9:

10:

11:

12:

13:

What are some things in the Lord's prayer that you find easy to pray?

What are some things in the Lord's prayer that you find difficult to pray?

If you find it hard to know what to pray for or how to pray, here is a simple pattern:
- Give thanks to God for who he is and what he has done.
- Pray for the needs of others.
- Pray for your needs.

Putting it into practice!

Pray: Share some concerns you have and pray for them in the group.

Think: About meeting regularly with one or two other people to pray together.

Think: About writing down your prayer requests in a book so you can remember what to pray for and also see how God answers each prayer over time.

Leader's notes
Heaven

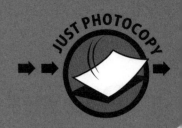

Individual studies

Aim) At the end of the study the young people should be able to say what heaven is like and that only a person who trusts in Jesus goes there.

Share The two opening questions will get people thinking about what they believe as well as help you discover how each person thinks about the subject.

A quick quiz Each person quietly goes through each statement and circles the answer they believe is true. When everyone is finished, discuss their answers. Some of the questions you can answer 'true' or 'false' and some you can only speculate. The study should answer many questions. Some biblical principles to work from are: God is good, only good things will be in heaven, God wills that all people trust in Him and go to heaven.

What I hope heaven will be like more than anything is: There is no right or wrong answer here but encourage them to think about either good things they experience on earth and want to see continue in heaven (eg relationships) or bad things on earth they hope to have 'fixed' in heaven (eg death, pain, bad relationships).

What does the Bible say about

... what heaven is like?
You may wish to read the whole of Revelation 21 for your own preparation. Some information that you may find helpful as you look at this section... • Revelation uses the Old Testament image of the city of Jerusalem as the picture of what heaven is like. It is a safe city where God's people live securely with God in their midst. • "New heaven and new earth" (v1) is a picture of a new creation (Genesis 1:1 - God creates the heavens and the earth). • "No longer any sea" (v1). The sea was seen as the place of evil (see 20:13) and in heaven there will be no evil.

Ask a volunteer to read Revelation 21:1-4. Ways in which this passage describes heaven: • New (better than the old). (21:1, 4) • No more mourning. (21:4) • God is with his people. (21:3) • No more crying. (21:4) • God will wipe away our tears. (21:4) • No more pain. (21:4) • No more death. (21:4)

Choose two volunteers to read the following passages: Revelation 21:27 Nothing evil or bad is there. **Revelation 22:4** We will see God.

... who goes to heaven?
Ask the group to tick the requirements they think are necessary to go to heaven and then discuss their answers.

Have a volunteer read John 3:16-18. Ask the group to choose only one item from the list of requirements above. Note that there is a difference between believing that God exists and actually trusting in him - even the Devil believes God exists (James 2:19).

... what we will be like in heaven?
Read the statement about our resurrection body. You do not need to read 1 Corinthians 15:42-54 now. This passage teaches us that our bodies will be permanent, glorified (this means made perfect), free from weakness, spiritual and cannot die.

Ask a volunteer to read John 20:19-20 and 1 John 3:2. After Jesus' resurrection his disciples recognised him. We will receive a resurrection body like Jesus did on the last day and will be recognisable to each other.

Think Challenge the group to think privately about their response to the first question. They may share their answers if they want to. Then ask them to volunteer answers to the second question.

Pray Spend some time in prayer.

Heaven

Share

What are some things concerning heaven you are SURE about?

What are some things concerning heaven you are not sure about?

A quick quiz: Circle your answer:
Y = Yes, N = No, ? = Unsure. Discuss your answers.

Y N ?   I believe there is a heaven.

Y N ?   There will be humour in heaven.

Y N ?   I think I have a good chance of getting there.

Y N ?   I'll be the same age as when I die.

Y N ?   I think it will be peaceful and quiet.

Y N ?   I think I'll be transparent and float.

Y N ?   I will see people I know.

Y N ?   It will be colourful.

Complete the sentence: More than anything I hope heaven will be...

There are many ideas and opinions about what heaven is like. However the only source that tells us what heaven is really like is the Bible.

What does the Bible say about

... what heaven is like? Read: Revelation 21:1-4
Using this passage, describe what heaven will be like.

Here are some other passages which talk about heaven: Revelation 21:27 and Revelation 22:4

... who goes to heaven?
What do you think are the requirements of going to heaven?
Choose as many as you want from the following list:

❏ Being a good person.   ❏ Trusting in Jesus.

❏ Believing that God exists.   ❏ Going to church.

❏ Praying & reading the Bible. ❏ Being baptised.

Read: John 3:16-18. If you had to now tick the boxes above but had to limit your answer to only one requirement, what would choose?

... what we will be like in heaven?
The Bible doesn't say a great deal about what we will be like. We do know that we will have a new body different from our earthly body. (A helpful passage to look at after this study is 1 Corinthians 15:42-54.)

Read: John 20:19-20 and 1 John 3:2
What does this tell us about Jesus' resurrection body?

What does it tell us about our resurrection body?

Think: Do you feel confident that you will go to heaven? Why?

Think: What can you do for those you know who are not confident about going to heaven?

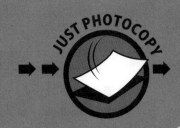

Leader's notes
Hell

Aim (At the end of the study the young people should understand that God is fair and punishes sin, but is also merciful and provides deliverance from sin and its punishment. This is available to all of them.

Be prepared later in the study for questions about people who have never heard about Jesus. Some passages for you to read in preparation are Romans 1:18-32 and Romans 9:1-20. Some basic biblical principles to work from: all have sinned, all deserve punishment, God is a fair judge and we need to make the good news about Jesus known.

Share Actions that deserve punishment. This exercise is to help the young people think through the issues of justice. Be prepared that some young people will not see any harm in some actions (like telling 'white lies', or doing things that don't hurt others like taking drugs on their own). You need to help them understand that all sin is rebellion against God. **Sharing questions** You may find that there will be a lot of questions about hell and maybe even some resistance to the idea of hell. Keep in mind that the study finishes in a very positive way showing that hell is avoidable.

What is hell and what is it like?

Ask members to read each verse and then draw a line to the words in the list that match the verses. You could divide into pairs and then ask them to share their answers.

Here are the verses with their correct match.
Make sure you emphasize the last one - that hell is avoidable.

Mark 9:43	Unquenchable fire
Matthew 25:46	Alternative to eternal life
2 Thessalonians 1:8-9	Punishment and shut out from the presence of God
Revelation 20:10	Prepared for Satan
Matthew 25:30	Darkness and torment
John 3:16-18	Avoidable

Lazarus and the rich man

Ask someone to read Luke 16:19-31, then read the statement about hell.
Note: When looking at this passage REMEMBER that this is a parable (a story that teaches us a truth) and may not necessarily be totally literal! For example, nowhere else does the Bible suggest that we can see between heaven and hell or converse with people from either place.

What is hell like for the rich man? A place of torment (v23 and 28) and agony (v24), permanent (v26-31).

Most people believe in heaven but why do some people refuse to believe in hell? You may have several answers to this question depending on what they have heard. However a classic answer is 'A good God would not send someone to hell!'. Help them to see that for God to be good he also has to be fair (remember the list on the back of the page when all were convinced that certain actions deserve punishment).

According to verses 27-31, what is significant about Abraham's answer? Someone DID rise from the dead - Jesus - but people still refused to believe.

Ask someone to read Colossians 1:21-22. It is our own sin that brings punishment. God is fair and punishes sin, BUT he is also merciful and provides deliverance from sin and its punishment.

What would you say to someone who is afraid of hell? Remember hell is avoidable: John 3:16-18. God punishes sin in his own son Jesus who willingly dies in our place (2 Corinthians 5:21). Jesus takes our punishment when we trust in him so we will never experience hell.

Pray

Share

What do you think are some actions that deserve punishment?
(You could make a list on the back of this page.)

Why do these actions deserve punishment?

The Bible describes hell as a place of punishment. Discuss the following questions:

What are some common views about hell?

What are the most difficult things to believe/ understand about hell?

What is hell and what is it like?

Here are a couple of things the Bible says about what hell is like. Read them and draw a line to match the description with the verse.

Revelation 20:10	Unquenchable fire
John 3:16-18	Alternative to eternal life
Matthew 25:30	Punishment and shut out from the presence of God
✗ **Matthew 25:46**	Prepared for Satan ✗
✗ **Mark 9:43**	Avoidable ✗
2 Thessalonians 1:8-9	Darkness and torment

Lazarus and the rich man

Read: Luke 16:19-31
Jesus taught about hell more than anyone else in the Bible. The story of 'Lazarus and the rich man' is a parable that Jesus taught that gives us some insights about hell. A word of warning: this parable does not say that rich people go to hell *last week* and poor people go to heaven - remember John *⤷ Trusting* 3:16-18. Hell is avoidable for everyone through a *in Jesus.* relationship with Jesus.

What is hell like for the rich man?

Torment
Agony

Most people believe there is a heaven but why do some people refuse to believe in hell?

In verses 27-31, hell is described as an avoidable place and the rich man wants to warn his five brothers. Abraham gives an interesting answer in verse 31.

What is significant about Abraham's answer?
(If you are stuck see 1 Peter 1:3.)

Read: Colossians 1:21-22
What is it that ultimately brings God's anger/ punishment upon us?

God is fair and punishes sin, but he is also merciful and provides delieverance from sin and its punishment.

What would you say to someone who is afraid of hell?

Leader's notes

Love

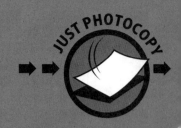

Aim At the end of this study, the members of the group should be able to distinguish between real love and the popular idea of love. Real love is seen in the active sacrifice that God makes for us, and we are called to do the same for each other.

Share Use this sharing question to get the young people thinking about how love is understood in our world. As the study progresses they will learn what the world says about love is not what God says about love.

How do you know when someone loves you? Ask the young people to make a list and when they have finished, circle the things that are ACTIONS (things people DO). This exercise is designed to bring out the fact that love is more than just emotional feelings. You cannot know that someone loves you unless it is shown in actions (actions include verbal action).

What is love like?

Both of these passages and questions below will show the young people that love can be a difficult thing to practice because it is not limited to those who are easy to love.

Choose a volunteer to read 1 Corinthians 13:4-7 Give the young people plenty of time to silently put their name to this list. When they are ready have them volunteer to answer what words were difficult to ascribe to themselves and discuss why. The next two questions lead into the second passage which talks about loving our enemies.
Discuss these questions.

Choose a volunteer to read Luke 6:27-31 Lead the group in discussion about how they respond to those who treat them badly and then talk about how this passage tells them to respond.

The example of God's love for us

Choose a volunteer to read 1 John 3:16-18.

Discuss the two questions about laying down our lives for each other. This may be a difficult teaching to grasp and you may need to explain that 'laying down our lives' for each other is about making sacrifices for each other.

The practical application in this passage is verse 17 about meeting physical needs of others. See if the group can think of any ways they need to do this for each other. You may know some ways that they can help each other out and have a list ready to share.

Verse 18 challenges us to love with action and in truth: don't just say we love each other, but do it. Again see if the group can come up with some ways to love each other in actions, and perhaps have a list ready of your own suggestions.

Choose a volunteer to read 1 John 4:7-12.
According to the verses below why should we love each other? You can do this exercise as a large group OR divide into pairs, answer the question for the three groups of verses and then share your answers as a whole group.
v7-8   It shows that we know God.
v9-11   God loves us so we should love others.
v12   We show what God is like when we love each other.

Pray

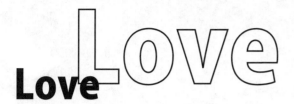 

Love

Share

What is a movie you have seen that is about love?

How do you know when someone really loves you?
Make a list:

Review what you have written above and circle all the words that describe ACTIONS (things people do).

What is love like?

Read: 1 Corinthians 13:4-7
Silently read through this passage and insert your name for each description of love (eg John is patient, John is kind, John does not envy...etc). **Which words did you find difficult to say about yourself?**

Which kind of people do you find easy to love? Why?

Which kind of people do you feel are difficult to love? Why?

Read: Luke 6:27-31
Love is not limited only to those that we like. This passage says we are to love all people, including those who hate us.
When someone treats you badly how do you naturally want to respond?

How does this passage tell you to respond?

The example of God's love for us

Read: 1 John 3:16-18
Jesus demonstrates his love to us through his death on the cross. This passage challenges us to do the same and lay down our lives for each other. **What does it mean to lay down our lives for each other?**

In what ways can we lay down our lives for each other?

What practical application does this passage teach us about showing love to each other? Can you think of ways we can do this for each other?

How can we do what verse 18 requires in our group?

Read also: 1 John 4:7-12
What reasons does this passage give concerning why we should love each other?

v7-8

v9-11

v12

God showed us what love is by sending his son who laid down his life for us. He loved us even though we did not love him. This shows us that real love is shown in action. We cannot claim to love someone and at the same time ignore them.

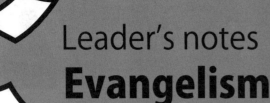

Leader's notes
Evangelism

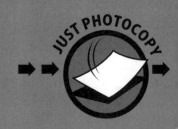

Individual studies

Aim (At the end of the study the young people should be able to express why evangelism is important and how they can share the gospel with their friends. This study is aimed at young people who claim to follow Christ.

Share Prepare members for the topic by sharing an example of 'good news' they have had.
Have someone read 2 Corinthians 5:21 and ask someone to explain what the good news is.
The good news is that Jesus set us free from sin and death through his own death on the cross.

Why do we evangelise?

1) God's word tells us to
You could look at the following verses a couple of different ways:
You could break them into pairs and have them look at all verses, and then come together and have individual groups report their answers; OR break into three groups and have each group prepare a verse; OR read them one at a time in the large group and share what the verses are saying.
1 Peter 3:15-16 Talks about being prepared to tell people about the hope we have and also how we should share this hope with others (with gentleness and respect).
Philemon 4-6 As we share our faith it makes us appreciate the good thing we have in Christ.
Romans 10:13-15 For people to believe the good news someone has to tell them (preaching means simply telling others).

2) The good news about Jesus saves!
Ask someone to read Romans 1:16-17: Then discuss the two questions. These questions draw attention to the fact that God can bring salvation to everyone - even those we may find hard to believe could become Christians.

Number the boxes: Have everyone number the boxes and then ask them to explain the reasons for their choice.

Share: This sharing time is intended to challenge members to think about opportunities to evangelise. It might be that not everyone will be able to share something (eg someone who has come to the group for the first time, someone who is not yet a Christian), therefore perhaps have an alternative question such as "how did you hear about Jesus?" Then ask what they find most difficult about sharing the gospel. The information below may help them with some suggestions of how it can be easier for them.

What can you do?

Read through the list below and give opportunities for response if time allows.
1. Gospel outline - you may want to have an outline ready to teach them. You may want to devote the next study time to learn ways to explain the gospel.
2. Look and pray for opportunities - you might give examples of opportunities you have had.
3. Remember that it is the good news about Jesus that changes lives - make it clear that evangelism is more than just living a good life.

Write the names of two people that you can invite to your Christian group or tell about Christ. You may want the group to share the names of the people they have written down.

Pray for the two people you have listed. You could have the group pray regularly for the two persons or remind them each week to continue praying for them and perhaps have regular updates on how they are going.

Evangelism

Share

What is one piece of good news you couldn't wait to tell people?

'Evangelism' is sharing the good news about Jesus with someone.

What is the good news about Jesus? (see 2 Corinthians 5:21)

Why do we evangelise?

1) God's word tells us to

God wants us to be involved in his work of telling the good news about Jesus. It is a great privilege to be involved in God's plan. What reasons do each of the following passages give for evangelism?

1 Peter 3:15-16

Philemon 4-6

Romans 10:13-15

2) The good news about Jesus saves!

Read: Romans 1:16
Are there people who you feel could never become Christians? If yes, why?

What hope for them does this passage give you?

The gospel (good news about Jesus) brings salvation!

Who do you find easiest to talk to about the gospel?
Number 1 to 9 (1 is easy, 9 is hard)

☐ Your parents   ☐ Your teachers

☐ Strangers   ☐ Your brothers/sister

☐ Friends at school   ☐ Christians

☐ Other relatives   ☐ Neighbours

☐ Other: _____

Share: Have you ever tried to invite someone to your Christian group or to talk to someone about Christ?
(If yes, what happened?)

What do you find most difficult when talking about Christian truths with someone?

What can you do?

1. Know what you must say and how to say it (perhaps learn a gospel outline).
2. LOOK for opportunities to tell people what you believe and PRAY for opportunities.
3. Remember that the good news about Jesus has the power to change lives. Therefore we have to do more than just live good lives, we must share the reason why our lives are different from others.

WRITE the names of two people that you would like to invite to your Christian group or tell about Christ.

1 _____

2 _____

Pray for the two people you have listed.

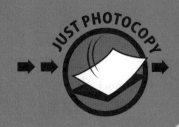

Leader's notes
Your group of friends

Aim (At the end of the study the group members should be able to recognise the positives and negatives of a peer group and how a follower of Jesus is to be different in the peer group.

Share About the groups that people belong to.

Write three words that characterise the groups and have them share their answers.

Identify the issues they face as Christians and how they are dealing with those issues. (Some questions that will clarify these issues are: Does being a Christian make a difference? Do your friends know you are a Christian? Can your friends see that you are a Christian?)

My group of friends

You want the young people to learn that belonging to a group is a natural and good thing. There are dangers however when the peer group dictates the way they live. It is important to learn what the Bible says about how they should act when with friends.

Dangers

1 **Your friends can influence you. Ask someone to read Romans 12:1-2.**
   Answer the two questions and discuss the problems they can face in conforming to their group and how they can deal with these problems. Remember that the group may at times be a positive influence.

2 **Groups of friends can be 'exclusive of others'. Ask someone to read Philippians 2:1-4.**
   Discuss the attitude of the group members to those outside the group, or newcomers.

3 **Your friends' acceptance can become too important to you. Ask someone to read Luke 9:23-26.**
   When your acceptance by others is more important than God you are tempted to do or say things that please people rather than God.

Tick the boxes

Instruct everyone to tick the box(es) that describe them best when they are with their friends. Ask the young people to share their answers and explain why they chose them. Share what boxes they did not tick and why.

Love

Ask someone to read what love is in 1 Corinthians 13:4-7 and Romans 12:9-21.
Encourage the young people to discuss their group of friends in light of these verses.

Pray for your group of friends and for yourself that you can be a positive influence on them.

What do you look for in a friend?

Friends
Your group of friends

Share

The best thing about my group of friends is...

It is hard to be friends with someone
The worst thing about my group of friends is... *when...*

> What three words would describe your group of friends:
>
> If you could change one thing about your group of friends what would it be?
>
> What activities or behaviour do you find hard among your group of friends because you are a Christian?

My group of friends

It is a good thing to belong to a group of friends that know and accept you, and with whom you feel you belong. Jesus had a small group who were closer to him than others (the 12 disciples). With any group that you belong to there are some dangers of which you must be aware.

Dangers: *!MAKE SURE THESE ARE TURNED INTO POSITIVES!*

1. **Your friends can influence you.**
   Read: Romans 12:1-2 (Don't conform means don't be like everyone else.)
   In what ways do your friends influence you?

How can you influence your friends as a Christian instead of conforming to what they believe or do?

2. **Groups of friends can be 'exclusive of others'.**
   Read: Philippians 2:1-4 (Looking to the interests of others means putting others first.)
   It's good to have a close group of friends but it is wrong if that closeness makes others feel unwelcome or that your friends will not accept someone new. **How good is your group of friends at welcoming/caring for new people or people who are left out?**

3. **Your friends' acceptance can become too important to you.**
   Read: Luke 9:23-26 Don't let your group of friends become your security so that your friends' acceptance of you is more important than God's acceptance of you. **Why is it a danger to rely on the acceptance of others rather than God?**

James 4:4
Friendship with the world.

Tick the box(es) that describes you best when you are with your friends, then share your answers:
- ❑ I can be myself.
- ❑ I can be honest.
- ❑ I speak up when the group does the wrong thing.
- ❑ I act/speak like a Christian should.
- ❑ I look after new/lonely people.
- ❑ I invite friends to church.

Are there any boxes you did not tick? Do you think this is a problem for you?

Love

Read what love is in 1 Corinthians 13:4-7 and Romans 12:9-21.
Does your group of friends reflect this?

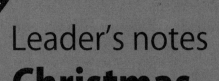
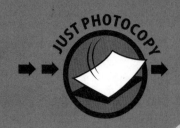

Christmas Themed Food.

Aim) **To learn the true meaning of Christmas.**

This study is designed to be shorter than the other studies as it is the end of year study. A suggestion would be to have a Christmas afternoon concluding with this study and prayer for everyone as they prepare to celebrate Christmas with their families. Estimated time for this study is 30 minutes.

Share Christmas is a celebration of the greatest gift of all, Jesus. These sharing questions are ideas connected with the study but intended to provoke members to discussion.

What does Christmas mean for most people today?

Ask the young people to tick the boxes of what they think people's views are. Listen to their answers and discuss them one at a time.

What does Christmas mean for you?
Ask the young people to write down what Christmas means for them, and ask them to volunteer their answers.

The Christmas story in the Bible

What are some truths you know from the Bible about the Christmas story? Either ask the young people to write down as many details from the Bible as they know OR ask them to raise their hands and share their answers spontaneously.

Readings
Allocate people to read the Christmas story from the Bible. It is a good idea to write down their names so that you can call their names one at a time. Some of the passages are only one verse but some are longer and you may want to break the larger passages into smaller sections. Try to encourage everyone to read - even those not as confident (give them the one verse passages) but don't push them if they are really resistant. At the end of each reading ask them to tick some facts they had listed previously. This also allows them some time to ask questions between readings if they have any.

a) Matthew 1:18-25
b) Luke 2:1-7
c) Luke 2:8-20
d) Isaiah 9:6
e) Matthew 2:1-12
f) Matthew 2:13-18
g) John 3:16

Christmas for the Christian

What is so important about Christmas for Christians? Talk briefly about why Jesus was born (he came to bring us into a relationship with God through his death on the cross to pay for our sin) and remind the young people that he is the greatest gift we could ever receive.

Pray This is probably your last study for the year so you should pray for each other for the holiday break.

Individual studies

Christmas

GAME? PICTIONARY

Share

The best Christmas gift you ever received.

If you could have ANYTHING for this Christmas what would you have?

What does Christmas mean for most people today?

Tick as many as you think:

☐ Presents   ☐ Shopping
☐ Stress   ☐ Family reunion
☐ Religious holiday ☐ Public holiday
☐ Santa   ☐ Myths
☐ Food   ☐ Annual visit to church
☐ Christmas cards   ☐ A time to be nice to everyone

What does Christmas mean for you?

Flip Chart

The Christmas story in the Bible

What are some truths you know from the Bible about the Christmas story? Think of as many details as you can.

Readings:
This is what the Bible records as the true Christmas story.

a) Matthew 1:18-25

b) Luke 2:1-7

c) Luke 2:8-20

d) Isaiah 9:6

e) Matthew 2:1-12

f) Matthew 2:13-18

g) John 3:16

Christmas for the Christian

The Christian celebrates the good news about Jesus. What is so important about Christmas for Christians?

Pray

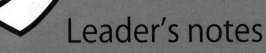
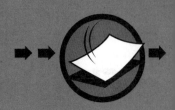

Coping with ...

Aim | This study will teach what the Bible says about how we should deal with conflict.

Share Introduce the subject in the sharing questions. Encourage everyone to answer both questions.

Put a cross on the scale Ask everyone in the group to put a cross on the scale which best describes them regarding each issue. Discuss their answers by using the question: **How do you want to be different?** Don't rush past this section if people want to discuss conflict they are having with those on the list.

The ideal

Read the three points out loud. You do not need to read the Bible references unless you would like to. Make any additional comments you would like to and make sure everyone understands these three statements before moving on. NOTE: For your information, Psalm 133 introduces the idea of unity being like oil poured on the head. In the Middle East which is hot and dry, oil was cool and soothing. Read the sentence about dealing with conflict.

Resolving conflict

Encourage everyone to write in their own words the advice the verses below give about conflict. Here are answers if you need them.

What advice is given in the following verses regarding conflict with each other?

James 1:19-20	Be quick to listen, slow to speak, slow to become angry.
Proverbs 15:1	A gentle word will help the situation, but a harsh word will make it worse.
Ephesians 4:26	Don't do the wrong thing when you are angry, sort it out before the day ends.
Colossians 3:13	Be patient with each other and forgive grievances you have against each other.
Romans 12:19-21	Don't take revenge, but be loving to your enemies.
Luke 6:27-31	Love your enemies, turn the other cheek, do to them what you would want them to do to you.

Is any of the advice above difficult to follow? (If so, why?) Encourage young people to share what they think would be difficult to do and why.

Ask a volunteer to read Romans 12:18. This passage makes it clear that we cannot control what others do, but we can control our own actions. We can therefore do whatever is in our power to live at peace with others. Discuss any issues raised by this passage.

What advice would you give to someone who...

Using the verses covered in this study, encourage the group to offer advice to the four situations. You could have the group choose which ones they would like to discuss.

Pray If there are some conflict situations, spend some time praying for them and any other needs.

Coping with conflict

Share

What are some things people often fight about? OR something you have fought about?

What is the worst outcome of conflict with someone?

For each sentence below put a cross on the scale that best describes you then discuss your answers:

I have conflict with my friends.

Always   Sometimes   Never

1 _____ 10

I have conflict with my parents.

Always   Sometimes   Never

1 _____ 10

I have conflict with my brother/sister.

Always   Sometimes   Never

1 _____ 10

I have conflict with teachers.

Always   Sometimes   Never

1 _____ 10

I avoid conflict.

Always   Sometimes   Never

1 _____ 10

How do you want to be different?

The ideal

The Bible tells us to:
Love one another (John 13:35). **Forgive as God forgives you** (Matthew 18:21-35). **Live together in unity!** (Psalm 133). We live in a fallen (sinful) world and, although the Bible teaches us to love and forgive each other, it also teaches us that conflicts are bound to occur and we need to resolve them as Christians.

Resolving conflict

Write in your own words the advice given in the following verses regarding conflict with each other.

James 1:19-20

Proverbs 15:1

Ephesians 4:26

Colossians 3:13

Romans 12:19-21

Luke 6:27–31

Is any of the advice above difficult to follow? (If so, why?)

Living at peace with one another is difficult if one makes an effort but others do not.

Read: Romans 12:18. What does this passage teach about this kind of situation?

What advice would you give to someone who

...is afraid to face conflict?

...has someone making life hard for them "for no reason"?

...has done everything to be reconciled but the other person refuses?

...is having conflict with someone and knows themself to be in the wrong?

Pray

Coping with parents

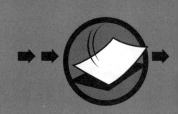

Aim (This study should give the young people in your group an opportunity to talk about some of the issues they face in their own homes. It should make them aware of their responsibility towards their parents and help them understand what God requires of them.

Note Be aware that some young people may have parents who do not treat them well, in which case you need to help them think through what respect and obedience will mean for them in a practical way. The 'advice' section should help you raise this issue and the section on 'God as Father' will give comfort to those who may feel abandoned by their parents.

Share Encourage everyone to answer both questions. The first question will help them identify a good quality of their parent/s which will set a positive tone for the study. The second question will help identify things that may be a struggle or point of contention with their parents.

Complete the exercise then share your answers. You could work through each question and have people volunteer their answers OR simply have them volunteer answers for the following questions: **Which statements above do you feel good about? Which area would you like to improve on?**

Parents and children

Ask people to volunteer to give their opinions on the following questions:
Why do you think God gives us parents? What makes a parent a 'good parent'?
Ask for four volunteers to read the passages that describe qualites of good parents. The passages from 1 Thessalonians are talking about how the Apostle Paul compared himself with good parents as he cared for the people at Thessalonica. You may like to note that a quality of a loving father is that he disciplines his children, Hebrews 12:7-12 is another helpful passage you may like to look at that talks about discipline. You may also want to ask what things would be important for a parent to teach.

What instructions do the following passages give to children?
Deuteronomy 5:16 This is the 5th commandment. Honour (ie respect) your parents.
Colossians 3:20 (cf Ephesians 6:1-3) Obey your parents in everything. Note that this pleases the Lord.
Proverbs 6:20 Listen to your parents' instructions.
Two other verses are 2 Timothy 3:1-2 and Romans 1:30 where disobedience to parents is regarded as sin.

What advice would you give to someone who...

Share some advice for the various scenarios, keeping in mind the verses above. You can work through each question or ask the young people to choose which ones they want to give advice for. Allow the young people to share their own insights before you give your comments. Be aware that some of these situations are a genuine struggle for the young person to do what is right. Be prepared also that some of your time in this section will be purely giving the young person the opportunity to express how they are feeling about their home situations, especially with the issue of divorce and step-parents. Once you have looked at the scenarios, allow the young people to share any other situations they would like advice about when dealing with parents. **Some other helpful information regarding Jesus and his parents:** Between Jesus and his parents there was conflict and he was misunderstood (Mark 3:20-21). Jesus still considered the welfare of his mother. While dying on the cross he made sure his mother was provided for (John 19:25-27).

God our father

Ask three people to read **Psalm 27:10** and **John 1:12** and **1 John 3:1** Point out that God is a father to those who believe in him and he is a father who will always love them completely. This is good news for those who do not know their father or have in some way been rejected by their own parents.

Pray Share some prayer concerns regarding your own relationship with your parents.

Coping with parents

Share

What is one thing you will imitate from your parents when you are a parent?
Is there anything you will do differently from your parents?

Tick the boxes, then share your answers:	Never	Sometimes	Often	Always
I obey my parents.	☐	☐	☐	☐
I think the same way as my parents.	☐	☐	☐	☐
I fight with my parents.	☐	☐	☐	☐
I apologise when I have done the wrong thing.	☐	☐	☐	☐
I talk to my parents about how I feel.	☐	☐	☐	☐
I try to be a Christian at home.	☐	☐	☐	☐

Which statements above do you feel good about?

Which area would you like to improve on?

Parents and children

Why do you think God gives us parents?

What makes a parent a 'good parent'?

There is not a lot of information in the Bible about how to be good parents, but have a look at how the following verses describe some qualities of a good parent:

Mother: 1 Thessalonians 2:7
Father: 1 Thessalonians 2:11-12, Ephesians 6:4, Proverbs 3:12

What instructions do the following passages give to children?

Deuteronomy 5:16

Colossians 3:20 (cf Ephesians 6:1-3)

Proverbs 6:20

What advice would you give to someone who

...says his/her parents don't understand them?

...fights with his/her parents about Christian things (ie attending church, what the Bible says etc)?

...has divorced parents and has trouble relating to both OR has trouble relating to step-parents?

...speaks to his/her parents in a rude way?

God our father

Though we all make mistakes, as well as our parents, the good news is that we have a father in heaven who is perfect. **Read the following verses: Psalm 27:10, John 1:12 and 1 John 3:1**

Pray Share some prayer concerns regarding your own relationship with your parents.

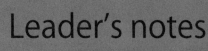

Leader's notes
Coping with worry

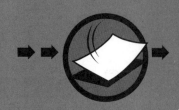

Aim (At the end of the study the young people should learn that worrying doesn't solve their problems. The study shows that God is in control of this world and that we should live in obedience to God and take our concerns to him through prayer.

Share The two sharing questions will help group members to reflect on worry.

What do people worry about most? Have the group spend some time ordering the list from 1 to 9 (1 = worries a lot, 9 = not so worried), then discuss their answers.

Which one of the above items do you worry about the most? Have the group volunteer answers about what they personally worry about the most.

Some advice from Jesus about worry

Ask one or a few people to read Matthew 6:25-34.

According to this passage, what are some of the issues that people worry about in life? Life - what they will eat or drink. Their body - what they will wear. (6:25-31)

According to the passage above, what does worry accomplish? Worry accomplishes nothing! (6:27)

Why do you think people worry in the first place (What do people fear)? Ask the young people to give their opinions about why people worry or even share the reasons why they themselves worry.

Note: people are afraid when they are not in control of their circumstances as suggested in this Bible passage.

How does this passage give us comfort about our worry? God is in control of our circumstances and he is a father who cares about us and provides for us.

Instead of worrying the the Bible commands the Christian to seek first God's kingdom and righteousness (6:33). **How do we do this?** Make sure everyone understands what 6:33 means. Seeking God's kingdom and his righteousness putting God first in everything we do. Think about examples of how we can do this. You may want to think of some of your own examples beforehand.

What advice would you give to someone who...

Share advice for the three situations, keeping in mind that we want obedience to God as our first priority. For example, if someone wrongs us, we would want to deal with the situation in a way that shows we are Christian.

Prayer

Note: Sometimes the things we worry about are too big for us to cope with. Suggest to the young people that it is helpful to share things we are worried about with mature people who can perhaps help us to work out some ways to handle our worries. Make it clear that some things we worry about requires help from others. For example if a young person is depressed, he/she should seek help from other people.

Choose one or a few people to read Philippians 4:4-7.

Make a list of issues that people in this group are worried about, then spend some time praying for them.

Coping with worry

Share

What is the silliest thing you have ever worried about?

Talk about a time when you were worried but everything turned out OK.

What do people worry about most?

Rate in order of 1-9 (1= worries a lot, 9=not so worried), then discuss your answers.

- [ ] Money
- [ ] Having a boyfriend/ girlfriend
- [ ] Family
- [ ] Death
- [ ] Other?
- [ ] Exams
- [ ] The future
- [ ] How they look
- [ ] Popularity

Which one of the above items do you worry about the most?

Some advice from Jesus about worry

Read: Matthew 6:25-34
According to this passage, what are some of the issues that people worry about in life?

According to the passage above, what does worry accomplish?

Why do you think people worry in the first place (what do people fear)?

How does this passage give us comfort about our worry?

Instead of worrying the Christian should seek first *God's kingdom and his righteousness (6:33). **How do we do this?**

*God's kingdom is where we live in obedience to God's rule. Righteousness means living in an obedient relationship with God or living according to God's standard.

What advice would you give to someone who

...is really worried every time they have exams or any kind of test?

...is worried about a relationship that is not going too well (eg they are fighting with someone)?

...worries about their popularity (whether people like them or not)?

Prayer

The right response of the Christian is to trust our worries to God and a significant way to do this is to talk to him about what worries us. **Read: Philippians 4:4-7.** Make a list of issues that people in this group are worried about, then spend some time praying for them.

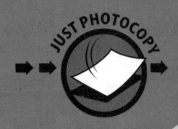

Leader's notes
A paralysed man

Aim (This study introduces Jesus to us as one who knows our hearts and is able to forgive us for our sin. His ability to forgive sin proves his identity as God.

Share The sharing question introduces the idea of power and authority and what it means. You may want to start with an example of your own.

Introducing Jesus

Answers to the Quick Quiz about Jesus:

He was an American	FALSE (he was a Jew)	He claimed to be God	TRUE (see today's story)
He wrote a few books	FALSE (he wrote nothing)	He rose from the dead	TRUE
He existed before	TRUE (ref John 1:1)	He was married	FALSE
He had blonde hair and blue eyes	FALSE	He travelled all over Europe	FALSE

(We don't know what he looked like but he was Middle-Eastern so probably not).

(he travelled only in Palestine).

Read the introduction to the next six studies so that the young people know what to expect over the next six weeks then ask someone to read Luke 1:1-4.

How can we know that the information about Jesus in the book of Luke is reliable?
Luke carefully investigated what he wrote. Luke gathered information from eyewitnesses.

Some words that may need explanation:
1) **Gospel** means 'good news' in Greek and so the gospel according to Luke is the good news about Jesus.
2) **Blasphemy** is claiming equality with God or insults directed towards God.

Jesus heals a paralysed man

Ask a few volunteers to read Luke 5:17-26.

What are some 'first impressions' you have of Jesus from this story?
Ask volunteers to share any observations or impressions they have of Jesus from this story.

Jesus said to the paralysed man, "your sins are forgiven" (v20). Do you think this is what the paralysed man's friends were hoping for? No, they wanted him healed.

Why were the Pharisees and teachers of the law unhappy with Jesus? (v21) He was blaspheming, claiming to have the power to forgive which is reserved only for God.

What is Jesus revealing about himself by claiming he is able to forgive sins? He is God in the flesh.

What was the purpose of healing the paralysed man? To prove that the man's sins had indeed been forgiven.

How does Jesus make forgiveness of sin possible for us? (A helpful verse is 1 Peter 3:18.) Through his death in our place for our sin.

Ask for volunteers to share: How would you feel if someone could read your mind?
How do you think people would treat you if they knew everything you were thinking?
Do you believe you are forgiven by Jesus? Have the group colour in the circle that expresses how they feel and then ask for volunteers to share their answers and allow the group to give advice. Point out that while sometimes we don't FEEL forgiven, loved etc, the Bible tells us that when we trust in Jesus we are forgiven, even when we don't feel it. Point out also that Jesus forgives us for all sin, even big sins.

Pray Share matters for prayer and pray together.

People who met Jesus
A paralysed man

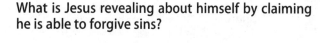

Share
Who do you think is the most powerful person alive today?

What makes them powerful?

Introducing Jesus

What do you know about Jesus?
Try this Quick Quiz:

He was an American.	T/F
He claimed to be God.	T/F
He wrote a few books.	T/F
He rose from the dead.	T/F
He existed before his birth in Bethlehem.	T/F
He was married.	T/F
He had blonde hair and blue eyes.	T/F
He travelled all over Europe.	T/F

The four Gospels (Matthew, Mark, Luke and John) give us information about who Jesus is. Over the next six studies we will meet Jesus as we read about him and those who came into contact with him in the Gospel of Luke. We will understand who he is, why he came and what he requires from us.

Read: Luke 1:1-4
How can we know that the information about Jesus in the book of Luke is reliable?

Jesus heals a paralysed man
Read: Luke 5:17-26
What are some 'first impressions' you have of Jesus from this story?

Jesus said to the paralysed man, "your sins are forgiven" (v20). Do you think this is what the paralysed man's friends were hoping for?

Why were the Pharisees and teachers of the law unhappy with Jesus? (v21)

What is Jesus revealing about himself by claiming he is able to forgive sins?

What was the purpose of healing the paralysed man?

How does Jesus make forgiveness of sin possible for us? (A helpful verse is 1 Peter 3:18.)

In this story Jesus knows the heart of the paralysed man (v20 – he is a sinner) and the hearts of those sitting in the room (v22). How would you feel if someone could read your mind?

How do you think people would treat you if they knew everything you were thinking?

Jesus sees your heart and knows everything you have thought and done and yet he offers love and forgiveness. Romans 5:8 says "while we were still sinners, Christ died for us". Do you believe you are forgiven by Jesus? Colour in the circle to show the number that represents what you feel.

I feel there are some things for which I can never be forgiven.
(No) O O O O O O O O O O (Yes)

I know that Jesus always loves me even when I've sinned.
(No) O O O O O O O O O O (Yes)

I sometimes feel I don't deserve forgiveness.
(No) O O O O O O O O O O (Yes)

I believe I am forgiven and going to heaven.
(No) O O O O O O O O O O (Yes)

Discuss your answers and help each other with advice in the areas where people feel they need help.

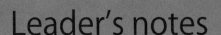

Leader's notes
A demon-possessed man

Aim (This study will teach the young people that while demons exist and can affect people's lives, Jesus has power over demons and so the Christian need not fear what demons can do.

Share Introduce the subject of fear and scary things through the sharing question. They may answer what they believe people to be afraid of or share something that they fear. Try not to discuss demons at this point. You may like to start with an example such as, 'many people fear spiders'.

What do you believe about demons?

This section is to give you information about what the group members believe and feel about demons. Ask the group to individually circle words that they associate with demons and then discuss their answers. Then have the group members tick the spaces that match their thoughts on demons and then share their answers. Feel free to spend some time discussing their answers.

Jesus heals a demon-possessed man

Ask for some volunteers to read Luke 8:26-33. What are some things we learn about demons from this story? Ask the young people to share their observations about demons from this passage. If they don't pick up everything, that doesn't matter, you can add what they miss. Here are some observations: they can take possession of someone's life; they are destructive (they hurt the man and destroyed the pigs); they are afraid of Jesus (they knew he could torture and destroy them); they recognise that Jesus is the Son of God; they are obedient to Jesus (they did what he told them and answered his questions); they are under the control of Jesus (they asked permission to go into the pigs).

How did the demons affect the man possessed? (In what ways was his life affected?) Ask the young people to share their observations about how the man was affected. Here are some observations: he was naked (v27); he was not in control of himself (v28-29); he lived among the dead in the tombs (v27); he lived alone (v29).

Why are demons afraid of Jesus? Jesus has control over them and can destroy them when he wishes. **What would you say to someone who is trying to get involved in the spiritual world through seances, witchcraft, ouiji (pronounced weegee) boards etc?** Ask the young people how they would advise people. When we read this story we see that the demons are destructive and evil and we want to warn people from desiring involvement with them through spiritual practices. We want to direct people to the spiritual one who is all-powerful – Jesus.

Responses to Jesus

Ask a few volunteers to read Luke 8:32-39.
How did the following people respond to Jesus in this story?
The demons (v28, 31-32): Acknowledged who Jesus is and obeyed his commands. **The people with the pigs and the people living in the region (v34, 36-37):** The people with the pigs told everyone how the demon-possessed man had been cured. Everyone was afraid and asked Jesus to leave. **The demon-possessed man (v38):** He wanted to go with Jesus. **Do any of these responses surprise you? (Why/why not?)** Ask the young people to share if the responses by the different groups were what they expected and why. Some interesting things to note are: the people saw how Jesus had healed the man and yet wanted him to leave; the fact that they were tending pigs (an animal prohibited to Jewish people) shows they were not obeying God's law for the Jews; the demons acknowledged who Jesus is (see James 2:19). **Why doesn't Jesus allow the man to go with him?** He wanted him to go and tell his family about how his life was changed by Jesus. **What do we learn about Jesus from this story?** Jesus has power over demons. Jesus is the Son of God. **How does this story help a Christian with a fear of demons?** We don't need to fear evil spirits if we trust in Jesus.

Pray Share any matters for prayer and spend some time praying as a group.

Halloween..

People who met Jesus
A demon-possessed man

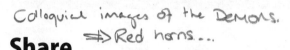

Colloquial images of the Demons.
⇒ Red horns...

Share

What is something of which people can be frightened? (or of which you are frightened?)

What do you believe about demons?

What words do you associate with demons? Circle any of the words below then share your answers.

Scary	Powerful	Ugly
Temptation	Hell	Evil
Interesting	Danger	Other? _____

Tick the spaces that match your thoughts: _____
When I think of demons I…
- ❑ Feel frightened.
- ❑ Like to talk about them.
- ❑ Think of comic strip characters.
- ❑ Feel curious.
- ❑ Don't like to think about them.
- ❑ Don't get worried.
- ❑ Think they are not true.
- ❑ Think of scary movies.
- ❑ Other? _____

Jesus heals a demon-possessed man

Read: Luke 8:26-33
What are some things we learn about demons from this story?

How did the demons affect the man possessed? (In what ways was his life affected?)

Why are demons afraid of Jesus?

What would you say to someone who is trying to get involved in the spiritual world through seances, witchcraft, ouiji (pronounced weegee) boards etc? *Horoscopes*

Responses to Jesus

Read: Luke 8:34-39
How did the following people respond to Jesus in this story?

The demons (v28, 31-32):

The people with the pigs and the people living in the region (v34, 36-37):

The demon-possessed man (v38):

Do any of these responses surprise you? (Why/why not?)

Why doesn't Jesus allow the man to go with him?

What do we learn about Jesus from this story?

How does this story help a Christian with a fear of demons?

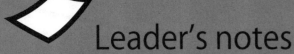
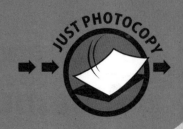

Leader's notes
A rich young man

Aim At the end of the study the young people should understand and be challenged by the fact that following Jesus means putting him before everything and everyone.

Share Ask the two sharing questions to introduce the study.

Ask the group to list in order of 1-10 which things would be hardest for them to give up/change. Discuss answers, perhaps ask what was the hardest and what was the easiest thing to give up and why.

The rich young ruler

Ask one or a few people to read Luke18:18-30.

Why was it hard for the rich man in this story to go to heaven? He loved his possessions too much.

The rich man believed that his good deeds would get him into heaven. What did Jesus say would get him into heaven? Giving up all he had to follow Jesus. NOTE: It is not our efforts (with humankind it is impossible) but God's efforts (with God everything is possible).

How do we do what Jesus asked? (How do we 'give up everything' and 'follow Jesus'?) This story asks us to put Jesus first. There may be things in our lives that we need to get rid of that prevent us from following Jesus. Discuss how people in this group can put Jesus first.

Why does Jesus say it is harder for a rich person to enter the kingdom of God in verses 24-25? (Think about the young man.) There is greater sacrifice involved for a rich man. Possessions, comfort, control etc can be a stumbling block to following Jesus.

In verse 27 Jesus says that 'what is impossible with men is possible with God'. How does God make it possible for someone to go to heaven? (Hint: 1 Peter 1:18-21) God sends Jesus to take away our sin so that we can know him. NOTE: The cost involved for God to forgive us our sin was his precious only son.

What will be the reward for those who put Jesus above everything in their life? See verses 29-30 – blessing in this life and eternal life in the next.

The cost of following Jesus

Using the quiz, identify those in the world that Jesus refers to as the rich. Often we have a wrong understanding of what it means to be rich. You may want to take a moment to allow the young people to make comments about how they feel about being rich if they answered yes to all questions. You may also want to comment on our need to be generous with our wealth. Regardless of our situations, Jesus asks everyone to give up everything to follow him.

What would you say to your friends if they said "it is too hard to be a Christian" or "you have to give up too many things to be a Christian"? Have the young people share their answers. Remind them of the end of this story, that the reward is greater in the end for those who choose to follow Jesus.

What could prevent you giving all of your life to Jesus? Have the young people volunteer to share things that they feel hinder them from following Jesus.

Pray Spend some time in prayer. Pray about the challenges this story presents to us.

Think Is there some way your group can get involved in caring for those who are not wealthy? Talk to your pastor or contact your local missionary society.

People who met Jesus
A rich young man

Share

If you could own any possession you wanted, what would you choose?

If your home was burning down, what possession would you grab as you escaped out the door?

List in order of 1-10 (1 = hardest, 10 = easiest) **what would be hardest for you to give up/change:**

- [ ] Everything you own
- [ ] Career choice
- [ ] Money
- [ ] Where you live (suburb/country)
- [ ] The way you speak
- [ ] The places you go
- [ ] Having a partner of the opposite sex
- [ ] How you use your time
- [ ] Good education
- [ ] Friends/family

Discuss your answers.

The rich young ruler

Read: Luke 18:18-30
Why was it hard for the rich man in this story to go to heaven?

The rich man believed that his good deeds would get him into heaven.
What did Jesus say would get him into heaven?

How do we do what Jesus asked? (How do we 'give up everything' and 'follow Jesus'?)

Why does Jesus say it is harder for a rich person to enter the kingdom of God in verses 24-25?
(Think about the young man.)

In verse 27 Jesus says that "what is impossible with men is possible with God".
How does God make it possible for someone to go to heaven? (Hint: 1 Peter 1:18-21)

What will be the reward for those who put Jesus above everything in their life?

The cost of following Jesus

Who are the rich people in the world? Try this quick quiz to see if you are one of the rich people in this world that Jesus talks about. Circle 'yes' or 'no'.

Is there more than one tap in the house you live in?
Yes   No

Do you have access to food at least three times a day?
Yes   No

Do you live in a home with two or more rooms?
Yes   No

Have you ever attended school/been educated?
Yes   No

If you have answered yes to all the above you are richer than 90% of the world. Jesus asks everyone in all situations to put him first but it is especially hard for those of us who are rich as there are many things that tempt us to live for our own enjoyment or our own fulfilment. **What would you say to your friends if they said "it is too hard to be a Christian" or "you have to give up too many things to be a Christian"?**

What could prevent you giving all of your life to Jesus?

A tax collector named Zacchaeus

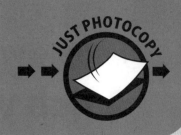

People who met Jesus

Aim (The story of Zacchaeus demonstrates that Jesus is willing to accept anyone. A clear sign that someone has understood acceptance by Jesus is that his/her life begins to change.

Using the list, ask the group members to place a tick in the space beside each quality they would choose in a friend. They can add other characteristics in the last three blank spaces. Once they have individually made their choices, have them share their answers.

What kind of person do you think Jesus would choose as a friend? What characteristics do you think Jesus would or would not choose from your list? Have the group members now compare their answers with how they think Jesus may have answered. Ask for volunteers to answer why they believe Jesus would have or have not chosen the same things. It doesn't matter if their answers are correct at this stage.

Zacchaeus meets Jesus

Ask for one or a few volunteers to read Luke 19:1-10.
What do we know about Zacchaeus from this story? Have the group share as much of a description of Zacchaeus as they can from the information in the passage. Here are some observations: he was a tax collector; he was rich; he was short; he was not liked; he was a sinner.
How did the people feel about Zacchaeus? They did not like him and considered him a sinner (probably because they had been robbed by him though taxes).
What does this story tell us about whom Jesus is willing to be friends with? (Think of Zacchaeus and look also at verse 10.) Jesus is willing to befriend someone who is not liked and is a sinner. It did not matter that he was rich. **Note:** Jesus befriends Zacchaeus before he changes and repays those he has wronged.
What effect does acceptance by Jesus have on Zacchaeus? He changes in the way he deals with people and his use of his wealth. He gives money to the poor and repays people four times the amount he has cheated them.
What similarities were there between Zacchaeus and the young man in the previous study (Luke18:18-30)? They are both rich and they both wanted to see Jesus.
How was Zacchaeus different from the rich young ruler? Zacchaeus did not approach Jesus about salvation but Jesus approached him. Zacchaeus responded to Jesus by changing while the rich young ruler went away sad. Zacchaeus was willing to give up his wealth.

Making changes

What are some signs that show someone has genuinely changed? Ask the group to try to think of some ways that prove a person has changed. You may want to have some examples prepared beforehand. One sign that someone has changed is their desire to repair relationships. Have the group members put a tick next to those listed who are easy to apologise to and put a cross next to those who are difficult to apologise to, and leave blank any that don't apply to them. Discuss their answers, asking them to explain why some were easy and why some were difficult.
Do you think it was difficult for Zacchaeus to make amends to the people he had wronged? Why/Why not? It may have been difficult because he had to make sacrifices (his wealth) and the people hated him. However, acceptance by Jesus may have meant that the sacrifices were easy.
Why is it important for someone who follows Jesus to be willing to repair relationships when we have wronged people? We need to show people through relationships that the Christian is different. We need to be willing to make amends to those we have wronged AND forgive those who have wronged us. These things demonstrate that Jesus has changed us.

Pray Share matters for prayer and pray together.

People who met Jesus
A tax collector named Zacchaeus

Describe the kind of person you would make friends with. What would they be like?
From the list below place a tick in the space beside each quality you would choose.

- ❑ Friendly
- ❑ Good looking
- ❑ Caring
- ❑ Smart
- ❑ Stands by you
- ❑ _____

- ❑ Funny
- ❑ Rich
- ❑ Common interests
- ❑ Athletic
- ❑ _____
- ❑ _____

Share your answers.

What kind of person do you think Jesus would choose as a friend? What characteristics do you think Jesus would or would not choose from your list?

Zacchaeus meets Jesus

Read: Luke 19:1-10
What do we know about Zacchaeus from this story?

How did the people feel about Zacchaeus?

What does this story tell us about whom Jesus is willing to be friends with?
(Think of Zacchaeus and look also at verse 10.)

✱ **What effect does acceptance by Jesus have on Zacchaeus?**

He did the opposite of what he'd been doing.

What similarities were there between Zacchaeus and the young man in the previous study (Luke18:18-30)?

Other stories to think about:
Levi ✱.
A Man with a withered hand
Centurions Servant
Sinful Women
Women & Jairus' Daughter

How was Zacchaeus different from the rich young ruler?

Healing a Boy.
Martha & Mary
Blind Beggar

✱ Making changes

What are some signs that show someone has genuinely changed?

One sign that shows Zacchaeus had changed was his desire to apologise by paying back all those from whom he had stolen. To whom do you find it easy to apologise? **In the boxes below put a tick next to those who are easy to apologise to and put a cross next to those who are difficult to apologise to.** (Leave blank any that don't apply to you, ie you may not have a job so don't have a boss).

- ❑ Mother
- ❑ Teacher
- ❑ Father
- ❑ Boss
- ❑ Sister
- ❑ Co-worker

- ❑ Brother
- ❑ Best friend
- ❑ Relative
- ❑ School friends
- ❑ Neighbour
- ❑ An enemy

Discuss your answers, explaining why you put a tick next to some and not others.

Do you think it was difficult for Zacchaeus to make amends to the people he had wronged? Why/Why not?

Why is it important for someone who follows Jesus to be willing to repair relationships when we have wronged people?

x How do you know that Jesus accept exc accepts you? Is it because you're smart, caring, good looking, friendly, funny or is it because explot this are...

x Do you accept people like Jesus does?

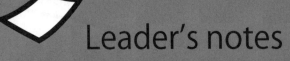

Leader's notes
A condemned criminal

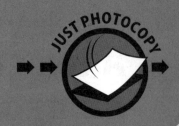

Aim ⎞ At the end of the study the young people should understand why Jesus died and how his death impacts us. They will understand that the forgiveness that Jesus offers is a free gift (grace).

Share Ask everyone to answer the sharing question.
Read the two scenarios and ask for volunteers to answer how they would feel in each situation.

What are the problems in each of these two scenarios?
Scenario 1: The friend wanted to earn the gift and did not accept it as a gift. They wanted to deserve it.
Scenario 2: The parents expected to be repaid for the gift, which no longer makes it a gift. A gift, by its nature, is free, there are no strings attached.

The condemned criminal

Read the paragraph about Jesus and the religious leaders.
Ask for one or a few volunteers to read Luke 23:32-43.

How did most people in this passage respond to Jesus? They were mocking him and abusing him.

What did the first criminal (v39) **want from Jesus?** He wanted Jesus to get him out of his situation.

Why did the second criminal (v40-43) **respond to Jesus differently?** He knew he deserved to be punished and that Jesus was innocent. He recognised who Jesus was and wanted him to save (forgive) him.

What do the words of the second criminal reveal to us about Jesus? That Jesus was innocent and did not deserve to die.

The second criminal received the free gift of forgiveness from Jesus. How was the gift of forgiveness given to the criminal different from the gifts given in Scenario 1 and Scenario 2? The gift of forgiveness was free and undeserved. It is different from the gift given in Scenario 1 because the criminal could do nothing to earn his forgiveness. It is different from the gift in Scenario 2 because Jesus did not ask for anything in return.

Read the statement about Jesus' death and make sure everyone understands it.
Then ask for one or a few volunteers to read Ephesians 2:1-10.

Note: 'Grace' means undeserved favour. It is receiving something as a gift that you cannot earn or deserve.

Advice

Based on today's story and the passage in Ephesians, what advice would you give to someone who…? Allow the young people to offer advice, keeping in mind a few principles: God has demonstrated his love for us in Jesus' death, through which we have forgiveness of sin. God's forgiveness is not based on our good deeds. We still do good deeds as a response to being forgiven, not in order to be forgiven. In regards to the last statement, we cannot fool God, he knows whether or not we have put our trust in him and there is no guarantee we will have that chance at the last moment. If we truly know God loves and forgives us we will give our lives to him. Forgiveness is not based on our good works but his mercy.

Note The criminal put his trust in Jesus but was not able to live a life of change as he was about to die. However, Zacchaeus in the previous study (Luke 19:1-10) was able to demonstrate his change of heart by the way his life changed.

Pray Share some matters for prayer and then pray.

Studies-2-go   For the leader on the run

People who met Jesus
A condemned criminal

Share

What is one nice thing you have done for someone else?

Spontaneous Drama?

Read the two scenarios below and share how you would feel in each situation:

Scenario 1: You buy your friend an expensive present for their birthday and they want to give you money to cover the cost.

Scenario 2: Your parents gave you an expensive gift and then ask you to work to earn money to pay it off.

What are the problems in each of these two scenarios?

Bible Noughts & Crosses? ↓ 9 Qs.

The condemned criminal

Jesus was a popular guy, however he was not popular with everyone who met him. The religious leaders of his day were jealous of his popularity and by the end of the Gospel of Luke, in chapters 22-23, they have him arrested and sentenced to death by crucifixion on a cross.

Read: Luke 23:32-43
How did most people in this passage respond to Jesus?

What did the first criminal (v39) **want from Jesus?**

Why did the second criminal (v40-43) **respond to Jesus differently?**

Q&A here. ↓
What do the words of the second criminal reveal to us about Jesus?

The second criminal received the free gift of forgiveness from Jesus. How was the gift of forgiveness given to the criminal different from the gifts given in Scenario 1 and Scenario 2?

cf 9:22

Jesus' plan was always to die. It was through his death that our sin was paid for. He was innocent (v41) but we, like the criminal, are guilty of sin (living our lives ignoring God). We deserve to die but Jesus willingly dies in our place. **To understand this more fully read Ephesians 2:1-10.**

KEY POINTS FROM THIS PASSAGE:
5-7 Min Talk.
✗
✗
✗

Advice
Conclusion:

Based on today's story and the passage in Ephesians, what advice would you give to someone who:

Feels that God doesn't love them if they haven't done enough good deeds?

Never does good things because they think it doesn't matter how they live?

Says they will live their life how they like and put their trust in Jesus just before they die?

Leader's notes
Two men on the road to Emmaus

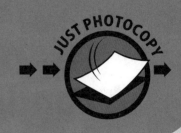

Aim (At the end of the study the young people should understand why Jesus died and rose again. They will also be personally challenged to think about what they believe about Jesus

Share Ask everyone to answer the sharing question. If they can only think of one thing they are sure about then that is OK.

From what you have learned about Jesus so far, what are some words you would use to describe him? They can write down the words in the space provided or simply share verbally. This is a review question, you could also ask them if they can remember who Jesus met from the studies and what they learned about Jesus from those encounters.

On the road to Emmaus

Ask for a few volunteers to read Luke 24:13-35.
What did the two men walking along the road believe and hope about Jesus? They believed that he was a prophet powerful in word and deed (v20). They hoped he would be the one to redeem (rescue) Israel (v21). **Note:** In those days Israel was under Roman occupation and many people believed that the messiah would be the one to deliver the people from the Roman oppression.

Do you think they believed what the women had said about Jesus rising from the dead? (Think about your answer and then look at verses 17 and 25.) They did not believe them since they were downcast (v17) Jesus says they are slow to believe (v25).

How does Jesus try to help the two men understand his death and resurrection? He uses Moses and the prophets (the Old Testament) to explain what had been said about him.

If Moses and the prophets talked about Jesus long before he was born (Moses lived more than 1200 years before Jesus!), what does this teach you about his coming? The death and resurrection of Jesus was planned from the beginning, it was not an afterthought.

Read 1 Corinthians 15:16-20. Why was it important that Jesus not only died for our sins but also rose again? Jesus resurrection was proof that he had conquered sin and death. If Jesus had not risen, we would still be in sin.

How were the two men's hopes in Jesus (v21) **fulfilled?** Jesus brought a real redemption, the forgiveness of sins.

Responses to Jesus

Use this section to allow the group members to reflect on what they believe about Jesus.
How would you respond to the following statements? Ask the group to share how they would respond. Encourage them to think about what they have learned in order to answer the questions. Some helpful comments on each statement are:

"I believe God is distant and doesn't care about our world or anyone in it." Jesus is the demonstration of God getting involved personally in our world.
"I will believe in God only if he appears to me in person." Jesus claimed to be God in the flesh. Even those who met him did not always believe. The Bible allows us to meet Jesus as we read about him.
"There is not enough evidence to know who Jesus is." The Bible is all about Jesus (even as far back as Moses and the prophets) and gives us eyewitness accounts of those who met him personally.
How sure are you about the following statements? Have the group members think about what they believe and circle a percentage. Ask for volunteers to share their answers.

Further reading: Since we can meet Jesus in the Bible, think about reading the whole of Luke in the coming weeks.

Pray: Share matters for prayer and pray together.

Studies-2-go For the leader on the run

People who met Jesus
Two men on the road to Emmaus

Handwritten: Cf 1:1-4. So that you may be sure of the things you have been taught.

Share

What are three things you are 100% sure about?

From what you have learned about Jesus so far, what are some words you would use to describe him?

On the road to Emmaus

Jesus had been crucified, died and was buried. It was now the third day and he had risen from the dead.

Read: Luke 24:13-35

1. What did the two men walking along the road believe and hope about Jesus?

2. Do you think they believed what the women had said about Jesus rising from the dead?
   (Think about your answer and then look at verses 17 and 25.)

3. How does Jesus try to help the two men understand his death and resurrection?

4. If Moses and the prophets talked about Jesus long before he was born (Moses lived more than 1200 years before Jesus!), what does this teach you about his coming?

Read 1 Corinthians 15:16-20.
Why was it important that Jesus not only died for our sins but also rose again?

How were the two men's hopes in Jesus (v21) fulfilled?

Responses to Jesus

The past studies about people who met Jesus allowed us to meet Jesus for ourselves and find out more about him. Use this next section to reflect on your own conclusions about who Jesus is.

How would you respond to the following statements?

"I believe God is distant and doesn't care about our world or anyone in it".

"I will believe in God only if he appears to me in person".

"There is not enough evidence to know who Jesus is".

How sure are you about the following statements?
Circle a percentage:

Jesus rose from the dead.
0% 10% 20% 30% 40% 50% 60% 70% 80% 90% 100%

Jesus proved he was no ordinary man.
0% 10% 20% 30% 40% 50% 60% 70% 80% 90% 100%

Jesus was God in the flesh.
0% 10% 20% 30% 40% 50% 60% 70% 80% 90% 100%

I feel that I know Jesus personally.
0% 10% 20% 30% 40% 50% 60% 70% 80% 90% 100%

Further reading
Since we can meet Jesus in the Bible, think about reading the whole of Luke in the coming weeks.

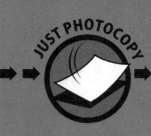

Leader's notes
Introducing the 12 witnesses and the Spirit

Aim ⟨ **This study sets the foundation for the book of Acts by introducing the Spirit and the 12 Apostles. By the end of the study the young people will understand who the disciples were and what their role was, and also understand that the Spirit is given to those who trust in Jesus.**

Share Introduce the idea of spreading the good news through the sharing question. You may want to point out at the end of the study that while there are many forms in which we could communicate the gospel today (books, television, internet), God often uses people to do it.

About the book of Acts

Read the section that introduces the book of Acts and ask if everyone understands it. **Note:** People often think the Gospels are about Jesus and the book of Acts is all about the Spirit. In fact, the book of Acts is the continuation of the work of Jesus by the Spirit.
Ask two people to read aloud Luke 1:1-4 and Acts 1:1-3.
From the verses above can you work out for whom Luke wrote this book and why? He wrote it to Theophilus. He wrote it to give an accurate account of the eyewitnesses to Jesus so that Theophilus would know the certainty of what he had been taught about Jesus.
How did he obtain the information for his two books? He carefully investigated the eyewitness accounts. Give opportunity for everyone to do the exercise by ticking the boxes to express what they think most people believe about the Bible. Discuss their answers by asking which boxes they have ticked and why.
How do the verses in Acts and Luke show us we can trust the Bible to be reliable? Luke tried to give an accurate account of what happened. He based it on eyewitnesses, not on his own opinion. He would have written it soon after Jesus since there were eyewitnesses who were still alive at that time.

The 12 witnesses and the Spirit

Read the section about the 12 disciples and ask if everyone understood it.
Think of as many names of the 12 disciples/Apostles as you can, and any information you might know about them. The names are recorded in Mark 3:13-19. If they don't know anything about them, don't worry too much. Some obvious ones are: Peter is the most talked about in the gospels and wrote 1 and 2 Peter; Matthew was a tax collector and wrote the Gospel of Matthew; Thomas, normally known as 'doubting Thomas'; Judas betrayed Jesus; John was the longest living disciple and wrote the Gospel of John, 1 and 2 and 3 John and Revelation.
Ask a few people to read Acts 1:4-11 and Acts 2:1-13. After Jesus ascended to heaven, what were the disciples to do? (Acts 1:8) They were to be witnesses (people who spread the news) to Jesus starting at Jerusalem and then spreading throughout the whole world.
How do you think the disciples would have felt after Jesus left them and went up into heaven? How would they have felt after the Holy Spirit came upon them? Ask the two questions about how the disciples may have felt before and after the Holy Spirit came. We do not know for certain how they would have felt but perhaps they felt a little sad to see him leave or nervous at the new task ahead. After the Spirit came they may have felt a peace that Jesus was clearly with them as he had promised.
Why do you suppose the Spirit gave the Apostles the ability to speak other languages? To have the ability to spread the message of Jesus to all nations. Ask the young people to volunteer their answers to how they would share the gospel more effectively with others and how they would describe the Christian message. **Ask three people to read: Acts 2:22-24; 2:32-33; 2:36-38.** Read the section about the Spirit. **Note:** Jesus now fulfils the roles of prophet (Hebrews 1:1-2), priest (Hebrews 4:14-15) and king (Mark 15:2 and Revelation 19:16). **Who has the Spirit now? See Acts 2:38 (see also Ephesians 1:13-14)** All who trust in Jesus. **Do you feel confident that you have the Holy Spirit? (Why/why not)** Encourage as many as possible to share their answers. This question will help make clear who in the group is a Christian.

Pray Spend some time in prayer.

The mission of Jesus in Acts
Introducing the 12 witnesses and the Spirit

Share

If you had to share some information with as many people as you could, how would you do it?

About the book of Acts

The Book of Acts is the sequel to the Gospel of Luke. The Gospel of Luke is the story of all Jesus began to do and teach. Acts is the story of all Jesus began to do and teach by the SPIRIT through the words spoken by the APOSTLES (the 12 disciples) after he ascended to heaven. The mission of Jesus in Acts was to continue to spread the good news about salvation to the world.

Read: Luke 1:1-4, Acts 1:1-3. From these verses, can you work out for whom Luke wrote this book and why?

How did he obtain the information for his two books?

Tick the boxes that you think most people believe concerning the Bible, then discuss your answers.

❑ The Bible is a bunch of fairy tales.

❑ The writers of the Bible wrote only what they think happened.

❑ The Bible was written a long time after Jesus so most of it is untrue.

How do the verses in Acts and Luke show us we can trust the Bible to be reliable?

The 12 witnesses and the Spirit

Jesus' 12 disciples became known as the 12 Apostles. An Apostle was someone given the authority by Jesus to spread the gospel (good news about the death and resurrection of the Lord Jesus). One of the disciples, Judas Iscariot, betrayed Jesus and then killed himself (Acts 1:16-18), so he was replaced by Matthias who had been a follower of Jesus (Acts 1:21-26). **Name as many of the 12 disciples/Apostles as you can (share any information you know about them).**

Read: Acts 1:4-11 and **Acts 2:1-13. After Jesus ascended to heaven, what were the disciples to do?** (Acts 1:8)

How do you think the disciples would have felt after Jesus left them and went up into heaven?

How would they have felt after the Holy Spirit came upon them?

Why do you suppose the Spirit gave the Apostles the ability to speak other languages?

If you could have an ability to help you share the Christian message more effectively with others, what would you want?

How would you describe the Christian message to one of your friends?

Peter gave a sermon after the Spirit came to explain to everyone what had just happened. His sermon gives a clear explanation of the Christian message. **Read some of Peter's sermon: Acts 2:22-24; 2:32-33; 2:36-38.**

When the Spirit came in Acts 2, it is not the first time he is mentioned in the Bible. The prophets, priests and kings of the Old Testament, who led God's people and spoke God's word to the people, also had the Spirit.
Who has the Spirit now? Acts 2:38 (see also Ephesians 1:13-14)

Do you feel confident that you have the Holy Spirit? (Why/why not)

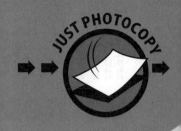

The new community

Aim At the end of the study the young people will know what the church at the time of the Apostles was like. The study will also help the young people to look objectively at their own Christian group and be challenged to make it the kind of group Jesus wants it to be.

Optional Quick Quiz A helpful way to start each study is to begin with a review quiz. See page 66.

Share Ask each young person to answer both questions to get them to think about the importance of belonging to a Christian group.

The new community

Ask one or a couple of young people to read Acts 2:42-47 to find out what the community at the time of the Apostles was like. **How would you describe this new community?**

Would you describe this group here like the one in Acts 2:42-47? Encourage the young people to share their impression of the community in Acts and then share whether they think this group here is like that. (You could also apply the same questions to their church or any other Christian group they belong to).

Ask the young people to tick all the characteristics on the list that are similar and cross those that are different between the group in Acts and this group here. Then discuss the question: **Are there any things on the list that you think must be done in a Christian group?** Some key features of a Christian group are prayer, teaching from the Bible, fellowship/love.

What was the result of the way the believers lived? (see end of verse 47) The Lord added to their number daily.

Our own community

In the box make a list of the characteristics of the ideal Christian group. They can do this as individuals and then share their answers OR agree as a group what should go on the list. Then answer the two questions on what they can do individually AND collectively to make their group match their description.

Is 'the Lord adding to your number'? (v47) Reflect on whether new people are joining their Christian group.

If yes, how welcome does a newcomer feel? Encourage individuals to think about what they must do to make a newcomer welcome (ie talk to them, sit with them, the group is not exclusive, the teaching is easy to understand etc).

If no, are there things that they could do to change it? Challenge them to evaluate their strategy in bringing newcomers into their group and making them feel welcome.

Further reading Since the book of Acts is such a long one, it is helpful to encourage the group to read some of it themselves each week as outlined in the further reading section. You may want to break the chapters up for them into a few sections to read each day.

Pray Spend some time in prayer.

The mission of Jesus in Acts
The new community

Share

What are some reasons why most people like to belong to a group?

What is one thing you like most about this group or your church?

The new community

Jesus has a mission to create a new community of believers. To find out what this new community was like at the time of the Apostles read Acts 2:42-47. **How would you describe this new community?**

Would you describe this group here like the one in Acts 2:42-47?

Here is a list of what is described in the passage. Tick all the boxes that describe this group here and cross those that don't.

❑ **Devoted to the Apostles teaching**
  (what we now have in the form of the New Testament)

❑ **Fellowship** (meeting together)

❑ **Breaking of bread** (eating together)

❑ **Prayer**

❑ **Signs and wonders performed by the** (12) **Apostles**

❑ **Believers shared their possessions**

❑ **They met every day**

❑ **They met in the temple and also in houses**

Not everything in the list need s to be the same between the group in Acts and this group here (for example, we don't have the 12 Apostles with us!). **Are there any things on the list that you think must be done in a Christian group?**

What was the result of the way the believers lived? (see end of v47)

Our own community

Describe the ideal Christian group (ie make a list of what its characteristics may be).

What are some things that you can do together to make your group like the community that Jesus wants it to be?

Is the 'Lord adding to your number'? (v47)
If yes, how welcome does a newcomer feel? If no, are there things that you could do to change it?

Further reading Read more about this new community in Chapters 3-6 this week. Also, if you would like a brief history of the whole Old Testament, read Acts 7. This section ends with Stephen being killed (he becomes the first Christian martyr). After his death persecution broke out and the church began to spread out from Jerusalem (Acts 8).

The conversion of Saul
(later known as Paul)

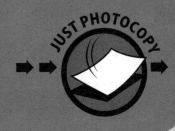
JUST PHOTOCOPY

Aim (The story of the conversion of Saul will teach the young people that God can save anyone, no matter how impossible it seems. At the end of the study the young people will also understand that becoming a Christian involves change.

Optional Quick Quiz See page 66.

Share Introduce the idea of 'change' with the sharing question. Every person should be able to think of some way in which they have changed, even if it is only something simple like that they grew taller.

Who was Saul (alias Paul)?

Read aloud the information about Saul to the group and make sure everyone understands it.

Ask the group to tick the boxes of the people they believe are less likely to become a follower of Jesus. The study will later teach them that God can change anyone. Some group members may already understand that anyone can become a follower of Jesus. If they come up with a new category they can write it in the space provided with the last box. Once they are finished discuss their answers.

Is there anyone you know whom you feel will never become a follower of Jesus? Why?
Ask volunteers to give their answers.

Saul meets Jesus

Ask a few volunteers to read Acts 9:1-22.

What was Saul doing before Jesus appeared to him? (v1-2) He was making threats against the Christians. He requested special permission to have Christians put in prision.

Why did Jesus say "why do you persecute ME" (rather than "them") in verse 4? Whatever is done towards a Christian whether good or bad is done towards Jesus. For further reference read the parable of the sheep and the goats in Matthew 25:31-46.

What does this teach us about the importance of how we treat other Christians? Christians are ambassadors for Jesus who share a special relationship with him. We are to treat them the way we would treat Jesus himself. Allow the group to give specific application to this question if they want.

Have you ever met someone who hates Jesus or Christians? If yes, how did you respond to them?
Ask the young people to share how they would have felt if they had been in the same situation as Ananias and then share about their own experiences.

What did Paul do as soon as he was converted? (v19-22) He spends time with the other disciples. He began to preach about Jesus.

You can tell that someone has become a Christian because they: Ask the group members to circle the characteristics they believe a Christian should display and then discuss your answers.

Do you think it is possible to become a Christian but not change from the way you were before? Why/why not? Discuss the group members' opinions. Help them to reflect on Saul's conversion, in that he could not remain as he was and still be a Christian.
Read aloud the section describing the change in Saul's life. Ask three volunteers to read
Romans 3:23, 2 Corinthians 5:17 and **Ephesians 2:8,9.**

Pray and recommend the **Further reading.**

The mission of Jesus in Acts
The conversion of Saul
(later known as Paul)

Share

Describe a way you have changed between now and when you were young
(eg no longer afraid of the dark).

Who was Saul (alias Paul)?

The Apostle Paul plays a key part in the mission of Jesus to bring people into relationship with him. The church had spread among the Jews (God's chosen people in the Old Testament), but now the Gentiles (non-Jews) will receive the good news and be included in God's people. Paul is introduced in the book of Acts as an enemy to Christians.

Look at the list below. Who are the people you think are less likely to become followers of Jesus?
(Tick the boxes.)
- ❑ Someone who doesn't believe in God (atheist).
- ❑ Someone who hates Christians.
- ❑ Someone who follows a different god.
- ❑ Someone who persecutes Christians.
- ❑ Someone who feels their life is OK without God.
- ❑ Someone who has committed murder.
- ❑ Someone who hates God.
- ❑ Someone who _____

Is there anyone you know whom you feel will never become a follower of Jesus? Why?

Saul meets Jesus

Read: Acts 9:1-22
What was Saul doing before Jesus appeared to him? (v1-2)

Why did Jesus say "why do you persecute ME" (rather than "them") in verse 4?

What does this teach us about the importance of how we treat other Christians?

Have you ever met someone who hates Jesus or Christians? If yes, how did you respond to them?

What did Saul do as soon as he was converted?
(v19-22)

You can tell that someone has become a Christian because they: (circle the ideas you think are right and then discuss your answers)

Look different.   Are always happy.

They treat others nicely.   Invite people to church.

Don't swear.   Read the Bible.

Talk about Jesus.   Meet with other Christians

Dress in different colours.   Eat different foods.

Do you think it is possible to become a Christian but not change from the way you were before? Why/why not?

God later used Paul to write most of the books (letters) in the New Testament. God is able to change us and use us no matter what we have done in the past. Have a look at some of Paul's writings in the New Testament:

What we were: read Romans 3:23.

What we are now: read 2 Corinthians 5:17.

God's grace: Ephesians 2:8-9.

Further reading: Paul goes on three missionary journeys to bring the good news about Jesus to the world. Paul and Barnabas' first missionary journey was to Galatia (modern day Turkey). You can read about it in Acts 13 and 14. On two occasions in the book of Acts Paul gives his testimony about how he met Jesus. Read about the first occasion in Acts 21:37-22:29.

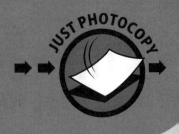
Leader's notes
The Gentiles accepted into God's people

Aim This study introduces the group to the issues between Jew and Gentile. By the end of the study the young people should understand that everyone is accepted by God on the basis of their trust in Jesus.

Optional Quick Quiz See page 66

Share Ask each person to answer the first sharing question and then ask for volunteers to answer the second question. Read the introduction to today's study and answer any questions they may have about what is written there. There could be some new concepts for them, such as Jews and Gentiles.

Have each person make two lists: i) people they accept and ii) people they find hard to accept. (eg people who.....treat me well OR treat me badly, who are kind to me OR are nasty to me). When both lists are finished ask the question: **Why do we easily accept certain people and reject others?** Encourage them to share their reasons. You could perhaps share from personal experience why you accepted some people and not others.

The Council of Jerusalem

The problem
Ask one or a few people to read Acts 15:1-11.
What was the problem? Some people were telling the Gentile converts that unless they followed the Jewish tradition of circumcision, they could not be saved. **Note:** At this point you may need to explain to them 'circumcision' (removal of the foreskin of the penis) if this word is unfamiliar.
What was wrong with the statement the men from Judea made in verse 1? (How is a person saved?) It is clear from the story of Acts that the Gentiles were being genuinely converted without the necessity of following Jewish tradition (see summary in box at the beginning of this study). A person is saved by believing the message about Jesus.
How does Peter respond to the men from Judea? God has shown that he has accepted the Gentiles by giving them the Holy Spirit and to ask more than this would be to burden them unnecessarily.
What is the basis of acceptance by God? Read Ephesians 2:8-13. By grace, the Gentiles have a relationship with God just as the Jews have, and this is through the blood of Jesus.

The decision
Read the section about the letter to the Gentiles. **Note:** The four guidelines given to the Gentiles were so they would not offend the Jewish people. Their adherence to these laws did not save them.
Why would it have been wrong for the Christian Gentiles to be circumcised? Their salvation was not dependent on following the law, but by grace (Acts 15:11). **Ask for volunteers to suggest ways we make it harder for people to become Christians today.** Some real examples have been: you must read the Bible every day otherwise you are not a real Christian; you cannot dance; an expectation that you will suddenly become 'perfect' (old habits disappear immediately).
Ask someone to read Galatians 3:26-28. What are some of the differences recorded here that exist between people? Jew or Greek, slave or free, male or female. **Can you think of examples when these differences become barriers?** Give examples such as issues that exist between men and women etc. If this is too difficult, make some suggestions and then move on to the next question.
How does faith in Jesus break down the barriers amongst Christians? He gives us an equal place before God so that one is not better than the other.
What can we learn from today's study about accepting each other? Take some suggestions of what this could mean practically for accepting each other. (Think back to the two lists at the beginning of the study about accepting and rejecting people). We need to recognise that we are all equal before God and that because God accepts us we ought to accept each other.

Pray Spend some time in prayer and suggest the further reading.

The mission of Jesus in Acts
The Gentiles accepted into God's people

Share

If you were to have any meal, any place, what would you choose and where?

What are some barriers that exist between people (eg rich and poor)?

The mission of Jesus is to bring people from all backgrounds into relationship with him. Chapter 8 introduces us to the first non-Jew (Gentile) converts to the Christian faith (Acts 8:4-40). Before that, all converts to Jesus were Jews. At this point the Jewish Christians had no policy about accepting the Gentile Christians as Jews did not associate with Gentiles (cf John 4:9). As the Gentile church grows through the missionary efforts of Paul and Barnabas, the question arises of how Jews and Gentiles can have fellowship, and whether the Gentile Christians should follow the Jewish law.

Make two lists:

Who are the people you easily accept?
People who.....

Who are the people you find hard to accept?
People who.....

Why do we easily accept certain people and reject others?

The Council of Jerusalem

The problem

1 Read: Acts 15:1-11
What was the problem?

2 What was wrong with the statement the men from Judea made in verse 1? (How is a person saved?)

3 How does Peter respond to the men from Judea? (15:7-11)

4 What is the basis of acceptance by God? Read Ephesians 2:8-13

The decision

The outcome of the Council was that a letter was written to the Gentiles stating that they were not required to follow Jewish law, but giving four guidelines to make fellowship with Jews easier (Acts 15:23-29).

Why would it have been wrong for the Christian Gentiles to be circumcised?

In what ways do we sometimes make it harder for people to become Christians today?

Read: Galatians 3:26-28. What are the differences recorded here that exist between people? Can you think of examples when these differences become barriers?

How does faith in Jesus break down the barriers amongst Christians?

What can we learn from today's study about accepting each other?

Further reading Consider reading the conversion of Cornelius this week (Acts 10). You could also read the book of Galatians, which deals with the same issues faced by the Council of Jerusalem.

Leader's notes
Paul the missionary and preacher

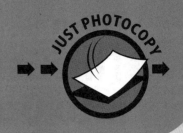
JUST PHOTOCOPY

Aim ⟨ This study will help the young person to understand the link between the Gospels and the New Testament letters through the book of Acts. They will also look in depth at one of Paul's sermons, the message he preached and how it relates to us today.

Optional Quick Quiz: See page 66
Share Ask each member of the group to answer the sharing question. The question introduces the idea of travel as you prepare to look at the areas Paul visited.

The missing link

Read the information about Acts being the link between the Gospels and the New Testament letters. Then do the exercise where they work out which books go with what locations. If this is a difficult exercise for them, allow them to have their Bible open. If it is an easy exercise you can simply have them call out the answer and also ask if they know which modern day country they belong to. Don't forget that some locations have two books named after them and are prefixed with a 1 and 2. They do not have to look up the verse references, these are only for future reference. You may want to have a map available for them to identify where these places are located. Some Bibles have maps of Paul's missionary journeys in the back cover. **Rome** - ROMANS (Italy); **Corinth** - 1 and 2 CORINTHIANS (Greece); **The region of Galatia** - GALATIANS (Turkey); **Ephesus** - EPHESIANS (Turkey); **Philippi** - PHILIPPIANS (Greece); **Thessalonica** - 1 and 2 THESSALONIANS (Greece); **Colossae** - COLOSSIANS (Turkey).

Paul preaches in Athens

One of the many places Paul visited on his missionary journeys and where he taught about Jesus was Athens, the capital of Greece. Here he preached a sermon. **Read: Acts 17:16-34. What is an idol?** Anything that replaces God. In the case of Athens the idols were carved objects that were worshipped.
How does Paul feel about the city being full of idols? He was greatly distressed.
Why do you think he feels like that? Ask the young people to volunteer their suggestions. This passage does not mention the reason, however, the message that Paul preaches shows that there is one true living God (see also 1 Thessalonians 1:9) who deserves our obedience, without whom we will perish.
How do you think God feels about idols? Ask the young people to volunteer their suggestions. The passage shows that God considers the worship of idols as ignorance and he now commands repentance (17:30). In the 10 commandments (look also at Exodus 20:4) God says he is a jealous God (ie he will not compete with other gods).
What are some things that we make into idols today? Thinking of idols as anything we put in the place where God should be, ask the group to volunteer some answers. You may want to make some suggestions to get them started or with which to conclude. Some examples could be: relationships with the opposite sex, possessions and popularity.
Looking at verses 24-31, ask the group to list as many things as you can that Paul told the people in Athens about God, including verse references. (Alternatively you could break them into pairs). Discuss their answers. Don't worry if they don't discover every point.
Information about God: God created the world and is Lord over heaven and earth **v24**; He does not live in a temple. **v24**; He is not dependent on humans. **v24**; He needs nothing. **v25**; He gives life and breath to all people. **v25**; He created everyone from one man. **v26**; He sets the time and place in which each person would live. **v26**; He is not far from any of us. **v27**; We live because of him. **v28**; God is not an image of human design. **v29**; He requires all people to repent. **v30**; He is judge of the world. **v31**.
What were the three responses to Paul's sermon? 17:32-34 - Some sneered, some wanted to hear more and some believed and became followers of Jesus.
Discuss ways in which a person can show that God is first in his or her life. Some examples might be to give up certain relationships that are unhelpful, to make choices that are difficult, to love people who are difficult to love.

Pray Spend some time in prayer and suggest the further reading.

The mission of Jesus in Acts
Paul the missionary and preacher

Share

Where is the furthest place or country from which you have received a letter or postcard?

The missing link

The book of Acts provides for us the link between the story of Jesus in the Gospels and the rest of the New Testament writings. After Paul was converted he travelled all over the Roman Empire preaching about Jesus. Many of the places Paul visited, he later wrote to. For example, he visited Thessalonica and later wrote 1 and 2 Thessalonians. Without the book of Acts our knowledge of the background to these books would be vague.

Below are the names of places that have New Testament books named after them. Can you write the name of the New Testament book (letter) after each place? (Some places have more than one book named after them.)

Rome (Acts 28:11-31)

Corinth (Acts 18)

The region of **Galatia**
(First missionary journey. Acts 13-14 and 16:6)

Ephesus (Acts 19 and 20:17-38)

Philippi (Acts 16:12-40)

Thessalonica (Acts 17:1-9)

Colossae
(Paul did not visit Colossae but once a church was established by someone else, he wrote to them. Colossae is the only place with a book named after it that is not mentioned in Acts.)

Paul preaches in Athens

One of the many places Paul visited and where he taught about Jesus was Athens, the capital of Greece.
Here he preached a sermon.
Read: Acts 17:16-34. What is an idol?

How does Paul feel about the city being full of idols?

Why do you think Paul feels the way he does about the city being full of idols?

How do you think God feels about idols? (Look also at Exodus 20:4.)

What are some things that we make into idols today?

Looking at verses 24-31, list as many things as you can that Paul told the people in Athens about God and write down the verse the information comes from.

Information about God (Discuss your answers.)

What were the three responses to Paul's sermon by those listening?

When we recognise who God is, a right response is to make him first in our lives. Discuss ways in which a person can show that God comes first in their life (rather than second place to an idol).

Further reading: Read about the missionary journeys of Paul. Journey 1: Acts 13-14; Journey 2: Acts 15:36-18:22, Journey 3: Acts 18:23-21:17.

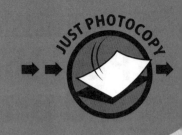

Leader's notes
Paul the prisoner gives his testimony

Aim ⟨ This study shows us how Paul took every opportunity to share the good news about Jesus. The young people will be challenged to have the same attitude.

The mission of Jesus in Acts

Optional Quick Quiz See page 66.
Share Introduce the story of Paul's testimony before a King through the sharing question.

Paul's testimony

Read aloud the section introducing Paul's situation at the time that he gave his testimony. It is helpful for your own preparation to read the chapters described here (21:27-26:32) before you start.
Ask a few people to read Acts 26:1-27 and outline in the space some of the key points Paul makes in his testimony (ie what does he talk about?). It doesn't matter if they don't put together a comprehensive list. Here are three key points for your group to consider:

Paul describes what he believed and did before he met Jesus. (26:4-11)
Paul describes his encounter with Jesus (26:12-18)
Paul describes the message of Jesus and what the right response should be to him. (26:19-23)
Considering what Paul said in his testimony, what things do you think need to be included in a testimony today? Ask the group members to give their thoughts on what should be included in a testimony. The focus of any testimony must be the work of Jesus in a person's life. Sometimes when people give their testimony they forget to even mention Jesus' name, however a testimony is ABOUT what Jesus has done on the cross for us.
Ask someone to read Acts 26:28-32. What did Governor Festus think about Paul? (v24)
He thought he had gone mad.
What did the King think about Paul? (v30-32) He realised he was completely innocent.
What are some other responses people have when they find out someone follows Jesus? Have the group members share some of their experiences of people's responses to Christians.
What would most people talk about if they were brought before the King accused of things they hadn't done? Ask the young people to think about what they would have said. It would have been a natural response for anyone to spend the whole time defending themselves against their accusers in order that they could be set free.
What was Paul trying to do when he was talking to the King? (Hint: v28-29) Paul wanted the King to be persuaded to believe in Jesus.

Your testimony

What do you think about the following statements? Have the group circle the answers they believe to be true and then discuss them.
What do you think is the best way for you to tell people about Jesus? Discuss your ideas. Some suggestions are: invite your friend to your Christian group; ask a friend if they have ever thought about what happens to you when you die, or other thought-provoking questions; ask the group what it was that brought them to faith in Jesus. This is an opportunity for the members of the group to think about how they can talk about their faith with others. Depending on the spiritual maturity of the group, you may want to have the group members write their testimonies during the week and have a Bible Study the following week devoted to listening to what they have written. This will only be appropriate if all claim to be Christians.

To be continued...

Read aloud the concluding paragraph about the Book of Acts, leaving them with the challenge to continue the mission of Jesus to share the good news with others. If you have some time you may like to have individuals share some things they have learned from the Book of Acts.

Pray Spend some time in prayer and suggest the further reading.

The mission of Jesus in Acts
Paul the prisoner gives his testimony

Share

If you could say one thing to the leader of your country, what would you say?

Paul's testimony

Paul was a key person in the mission of Jesus to bring the good news to the Gentiles. This however, had outraged the Jews, who had him arrested under false charges and imprisoned in Caesarea for two years. The Jews then tried to have Paul sent to Jerusalem so that they could ambush him and kill him on the journey. However, Paul was not only a Jew, he was also a Roman citizen. This gave him the right to have his case heard in Rome. Before he was sent to Rome he appeared before Governor Festus and King Agrippa to determine what should be written to the Roman emperor concerning his crimes.

Read: Acts 26:1-27

This is the second time Paul has told his testimony (story of how he became a Christian) in Acts. **Outline in the space below some of the key points Paul makes in his testimony (ie what does he talk about?).**

Considering what Paul said in his testimony, what things do you think need to be included in a testimony today?

Read: Acts 26:28-32. What did Governor Festus think about Paul? (v24)

What did the King think about Paul? (v30-32)

What are some other responses people have when they find out someone follows Jesus?

What would most people talk about if they were brought before the King accused of things they hadn't done?

What was Paul trying to do when he was talking to the King? (Hint: v28-29)

Your testimony

What do you think about the following statements? Circle Yes or No.

If you are a Christian you will want people to know about Jesus.   Yes   No

You have to know a lot about the Bible before you can tell people about Jesus.   Yes   No

It would be best to keep quiet about being a Christian if it offends people.   Yes   No

People will think you are a weird fanatic if you tell them about Jesus.   Yes   No

What do you think is the best way for you to tell others about Jesus? Discuss your ideas.

To be continued...

The story of Acts ends with Paul being sent to Rome for trial and concludes with him living in his own house preaching about the Lord Jesus. The ending to Acts leaves some questions unanswered, like what eventually happened to Paul and his trial. The story of Acts does not end here. The mission of Jesus to bring the good news to the world continues with us. We now are responsible for bringing the good news about Jesus to the people we know today.

Further reading: Read the remaining parts of Acts that you have not already covered.

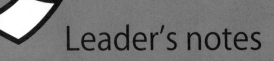

Leader's notes
Creation Genesis 1 and 2

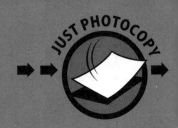

In the beginning ...

Aim (At the end of the study the group members should know that God created this world, and that he described it as 'good', and that he created us for relationship.

Share Begin with a sharing time to start discussion leading to the topic of creation.

Creation

Ask someone to read Genesis 1:1-2.
What do these verses tell us about the origin of God and the origin of this world?
Origin of the world = God.
The origin of God = no beginning because he is eternal and has no beginning.

To illustrate the concept of 'eternal' (without beginning or end) hold up two mirrors to each other and look in each reflection. The reflection in both mirrors goes on forever. Eternity is hard for us to comprehend as we are used to a world where everything has a beginning and an end.

Using the verse references of each day of creation, draw what was created on each day. This can be done in pairs or as a group.

How does God describe his creation? (v10; 12; 18; 21; 25) Good.

How does God describe his creation on day six (after humans are created)? (1:31) Very good.

According to Genesis 1:26-27, What makes human beings 'in the image of God'?
1:26 We rule. 1:27 We relate (We are male and female).

Creation take 2!

Ask someone or a couple of people to read Genesis 2:8 and 2:15-25.
This is a review of creation with a focus on specific detail - namely the creation of humans.

What 'creations' are the focus in this section? The creation of man and woman.

What is the first aspect of God's creation referred to as NOT good? (v18) Man is alone.

What does this tell you about the importance of relationship? God created us to have relationship and so we need each other. **Note:** Although God was with Adam, he wanted Adam to relate to another person - God has created us for relationship with him AND with each other.

Help the young people to consider how God would like them to relate to each other.

Is there anything on the list you think you need to work on? What are some practical steps you could take to improve at it? This is a personal question so ask for volunteers to share their answers. (Include these concerns in the items for prayer).

Ask someone to read John 1:1-5 and 10-13.
In light of Genesis 1-2, what does the passage from John tell us about who Jesus is? God/creator.

We were created for relationship especially relationship with Jesus. Who are the people that have relationship with Jesus? Those who receive him and believe in his name.

Pray Spend some time in prayer.

In the beginning ...
Creation Genesis 1 and 2

Share What is something you have made?

Creation

READ: Genesis 1:1-2
What do these verses tell us about the origin of
God and the origin of this world?

Read each day of creation and draw what was created
on each day.

Day 1 (1:3-5)

Day 2 (1:6-8)

Day 3 (1:9-13)

Day 4 (1:14-19)

Day 5 (1:20-23)

Day 6 (1:24-31)

Day 7 (2:2-3)

How does God describe his creation?
(v10; 12; 18; 21; 25)

How does God describe his creation on day six
(after humans are created)? (1:31)

Genesis indicates that people are special because
we are the only ones created in God's image.
According to Genesis 1:26-27, what makes human
beings 'in the image of God'?

1:26   1:27

Creation take 2!

READ: Genesis 2:8 and 2:15-25
What 'creations' are the focus in this section?

What is the first aspect of God's creation referred
to as NOT good? (v18)

What does this tell you about the importance of
relationship?

If relationship to each other shows that we are
in God's image (male and female - Genesis 1:27),
how then should we treat each other? Make a list
(perhaps on the reverse side of this page) of how
you think God wants us to relate to each other (eg
be patient). (Some helpful verses are: Galatians 5:22-
23, Romans 12:17-19 and
1 Corinthians 13:4-7.)

Is there anything on the list you think you need to
work on? What are some practical steps you could
take to improve at it?

READ: John 1:1-5 and 10-13

In light of Genesis 1-2, what does the passage
from John teach us about who Jesus is?

We were created for relationship and especially for
relationship with Jesus. Who are the people that
have a relationship with Jesus?

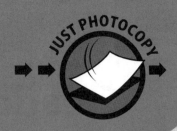

Leader's notes
Sin Genesis 3

Aim (At the end of the study the young people should be able to learn how people have ruined God's good creation, including relationship, but that God has a plan to forgive and reconcile people to himself.

Optional Quick Quiz A helpful way to start each study is to begin with a review quiz. See page 67.

Share Use the sharing question to introduce the concept of obeying authority.

Relationship suffers

Have someone or a few people read Genesis 3:1-13. How has the relationship between Adam and God changed in this chapter? (v8-10) Adam was afraid and ashamed of his nakedness (exposure). **How has the relationship between Adam and Eve changed in this chapter?** (v7 and 12) Adam and Eve are conscious of being naked and exposed before each other, unlike in 2:25. Adam also fails to take responsibility for his actions and blames his wife.
Discuss some ways which show that relationships have gone wrong with: a) God (think of examples of how we ignore and disobey God) and b) each other (think of ways we treat each other that show our relationships are not perfect).
In case you were wondering... Why was Adam blamed for sin entering the world when it was clearly Eve who ate the fruit first? (For example see Romans 5:12 and 17-19). God gave instructions about the tree of good and evil to Adam before Eve was created, making him responsible for her. Adam was with Eve when she was being deceived but remained silent. Adam's big failure was in listening to Eve rather than enforcing God's word (3:17). Eve's big failure was disobeying God's word through not listening to Adam. (However it is clear that she was not held responsible in the same way Adam was. See 1 Timothy 2:13-14.)

Discuss the three situations listed and show how fear has crept into our relationships.

Creation suffers

Have three people read the three curses in Genesis 3:14-19. What do we see in our world that shows us that creation is no longer the good place God originally intended? Share some things that show the earth is ruined by sin. Some examples are: People get angry with one another, wars, famines, divorce. **What is the most severe penalty for sin that all living things suffer?** (v19) Adam's relationship with the earth is disrupted and, more importantly, death comes through sin. **Note:** A common **question** about Eve's curse is about her desire for her husband and him ruling over her. A reasonable **answer:** Eve's desire will be to rule her husband (same Hebrew expression as Genesis 4:7 where sin's desire is for Cain), but the result will be that he will rule over her, suggesting a type of rule that is not desirable to her (maybe tyrannical rule).

God's mercy

Have one or two people read Genesis 3:20-24.
Adam and Eve disobeyed God but God still showed mercy. How did he show mercy? 3:21 Providing for them (clothes). **3:22-24** Banishing them from the tree of life so that they would not live forever in their fallen state.
Have someone read Revelation 21:1-3. Compare Genesis 3 with Revelation and write next to the Revelation passages how the new creation is different from the old:

Genesis 3	Revelation
Death enters through sin (3:19).	21:4 No more death.
People are banished from the tree of life (3:22-24).	22:1-2 Access to the tree of life.
People and the world are under a curse because of sin (3:16-19).	22:3 No more curse.

Pray Spend some time in prayer.

In the beginning ...
Sin Genesis 3

Share

What are some things ALL parents ask their kids to do (eg "clean your room")?

Relationship suffers

READ: Genesis 3:1-13
How has the relationship between Adam and God changed in this chapter? (v8-10)

How has the relationship between Adam and Eve changed in this chapter? (v7 and 12)

Discuss some ways which show that relationships today have gone wrong with:
a) God

b) each other

In Genesis 3, fear enters relationships. Discuss why we feel afraid when we:
Confess that we have done something wrong.

Talk to new people we don't know.

Tell someone that what they have done is wrong.

Creation suffers

Read: Genesis 3:14-19
Relationships with God and each other are not the only things that suffer because of sin - the creation also suffers. This world is now under the curse.
What do we see in our world that shows us that creation is no longer the good place God originally intended?

What is the most severe penalty for sin that all living things suffer? (v19)

God's mercy

Read: Genesis 3:20-24
Adam and Eve disobeyed God but God still showed mercy. How did he show mercy?

3:21

3:22-24

God also gives hope in the offspring of the woman who will crush the serpent's head (Genesis 3:15). He does this through his own son Jesus who absorbs the curse through his death on the cross. (Galatians 3:13). Through Jesus, broken relationships are restored and when Jesus returns for a second time, God will bring about a new creation.

Read: Revelation 21:1-3 and comparing the passages below, write next to the Revelation passages how the new creation is different from the old creation:

Death enters through sin (Genesis 3:19).
Revelation 21:4

People are banished from the tree of life (Gen 3:22-24).
Revelation 22:1-2

People and the world are under a curse because of sin (Gen 3:16-19).
Revelation22:3

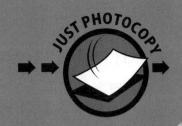
JUST PHOTOCOPY

Leader's notes
The spread of sin
Genesis 4 and 5

Aim ⟩ At the end of the study the young people will see the continuing effects of Adam and Eve's sin and recognise that there are two types of people: those who follow God and those who don't.

Optional Quick Quiz See page 67.

Share Ask the sharing question. There are a few passages to look at in this study so you may want to allocate readers at this point.

Cain and Abel

Ask one person or a couple of people to read the passage in Genesis 4:1-10.
What was it about Abel's attitude that made his offering better than his brother's?
(see Hebrews 11:4) He had faith.
When Cain's offering was rejected how did he behave, that is, what was his attitude?
(v5) He is angry and downcast.
God warned Cain to reject sin (v7) **but what happened in the next verse** (v8)**?**
He gives in to sin and kills Abel.

Discuss the question about dealing with jealousy and anger then look at the two passages.
What do the following passages tell us to do?
Ephesians 4:26-27 Don't let the sun go down on our anger – try to work things out.
Matthew 5:21-24 Deal with our problems with others as soon as we can.
Discuss how people feel about sorting out conflicts with others and whether or not they find they can do it. When we don't sort out our conflicts with others, the example of Cain shows us that it can lead to sin.

God punishes Cain by banishing him to be a restless wanderer (4:11-16). **In what way was God still merciful to Cain?** (v13-15) God still protected him.

What does this show us about God? God punishes sin but he still shows mercy to the sinner.

Two types of people

Read the section about Genesis 5 to the group and make sure they understand what is says.
Note: The geneaologies (lists of descendants) in the Bible can be traced from Adam to Jesus showing God's continued plan of salvation. These lists of descendants don't include everyone, but record only the people and details important to God's plan.

Note: A common question is 'who did Cain marry?' We see that Adam and Eve had more children – remember, however, a genealogy does not record everyone that existed.

Number the boxes: ask everyone to number the boxes and then ask for volunteers to explain their answers.

Discuss: Which do you find easy and which do you find difficult? Why?

What would you say to someone who claims he or she loves God but doesn't live like it? Discuss answers and then ask someone to read John 14:15 which clearly tells us that loving Jesus means obedience to him.

Think Read the question and ask them to consider this week which one of the two types of people they are.

Pray Spend some time in prayer.

In the beginning ...
The spread of sin
Genesis 4 and 5

Share
What are some things you have fought about with your brother or sister?

Cain and Abel
READ: Genesis 4:1-10
What was it about Abel's attitude that made his offering better than his brother's?
(see Hebrews 11:4)

When Cain's offering was rejected how did he behave, that is, what was his attitude? (v5)

God warned Cain to reject sin (v7) **but what happened in the next verse** (v8)**?**

What do you do when you are jealous of someone or angry with someone?

What do the following passages tell us to do?

Ephesians 4:26-27

Matthew 5:21-24

We have to choose to do what God wants us to do.
What happens when you don't deal with your anger or jealousy? (Think about Cain.)

God punishes Cain by banishing him to be a restless wanderer (4:11-16).
In what way was God still merciful to Cain?
(v13-15)

What does this show us about God?

Two types of people
Chapter 5 shows how sin continues to spread through the generations of Adam and Eve's children. The descendants of Cain were people who ignored God (eg Lamech, 4:19-24), however, a new line of descendants from Seth (Adam and Eve's third son) are people who followed God (eg Enoch, 5:21-24, Hebrews 11:5-6) and who began 'to call on the name of the Lord' (4:26).

> The person who follows God must be someone who is different from those who don't follow God. Rate out of 10 (1 = it is easy to be different, 10 = is hard to be different).
>
> **How do you rate yourself in the following actions as you try to be different?**
>
> ☐ How you speak ☐ Your thoughts
>
> ☐ Honesty ☐ Relationships with the opposite sex
>
> **How you treat your:**
>
> ☐ family ☐ friends
>
> ☐ enemies

From the above, which do you find easy and which do you find difficult? Why?

What would you say to someone who claims he or she loves God but doesn't live like it? (see John 14:15)

Think: There are two types of people: those who follow God and those who don't. To which group do you belong?

Leader's notes
Noah Part 1: The flood
Genesis 6-8

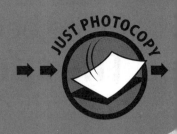

Aim At the end of the study the young people will understand the reasons for punishment of sin and the reality of God's mercy. The group would also become familiar with the story of Noah.

Optional Quick Quiz See page 67

Share Ask everyone to answer the sharing question.

The reason for the flood

Ask the young people to share what they know about the story of Noah and the flood.

Ask someone to read Genesis 6:1-7. You may want to pronounce the word 'Nephilim' for them. Read the section about the mixed marriages aloud for them and make sure they understand it. The Nephilim are mentioned only one other time in the Bible, in Numbers 13:33. Unfortunately, this passage does not explain who they were. There are different views on who 'sons of God' and 'daughters of men' were, and you may like to read a commentary that will explain the other options and present them to your group. Another common theory is that the Nephilim were fallen angels.
How does the passage describe humankind? (v5) Wicked, evil thoughts all the time.
How does people's sin make God feel? (v6) Grieved and filled with pain.
What two things does God decide to do in response to people's sin? (v3 and 7) Shorten their lives, and wipe them out with a flood.
Note: Life shortened to 120 years (Genesis 6:3) could mean their lives were limited to 120 years OR it was around 120 years later that God sent the flood and wiped them out.

The story of Noah

Ask someone to read Genesis 6:8-14. How did Noah find favour with God? (See also Hebrews 11:7) Noah found favour with the Lord because of his faith. **Note:** We also find favour with God through faith in Jesus, but even faith is a gift from God (see Ephesians 2:8-9).
Did the people of Noah's time deserve punishment? The people deserved punishment as the passage makes it clear they were sinful.
What was the punishment for their sin? Read: Genesis 7:22-23 Death through the flood.
Allocate readers to read the flood story: Genesis 7:1-4 and **6-12** and **8:1** and **8:6-12** and **8:15-22.**
You may want to encourage them to read the whole story themselves that week.
Covenant: The word covenant is included in the story (6:18) but not read in these passages. The word means promise and will be dealt with in the next study. **Clean animals:** The animals determined by God to be acceptable for eating and sacrifice. There is a list in Leviticus 11:1-47. Today we don't follow the Jewish list of 'clean and unclean' as Jesus has fulfilled the requirements of the law by being the one true sacrifice. Some passages about the Christian view of foods are: Mark 7:14-19; 1 Corinthians 8:1-8 and Colossians 2:16-23.
Answers to the true or false questions:
1. **False** 7:4 2. **True** 7:13 3. **False** 8:1 (6:18) 4. **True** 8:8-12 5. **False** 7:23 6. **False** 8:21 7. **False** 8:21

Judgment day

Read the section about the return of Jesus and make sure it is understood.
Ask one or two people to read Matthew 24:36-44.
What does this passage tell you about the return of Jesus? Sudden.
How can you be ready for the day that Jesus returns? Put your trust in Jesus.
If people deserve punishment and God warns us that judgement day will come, what should we do for others? Warn them!

Pray Spend some time in prayer.

In the beginning ...
Noah Part 1: The flood
Genesis 6-8

Share
If you could go anywhere on a cruise, where would you go?

The reason for the flood
What do you know about the story of Noah and the flood?

Read: Genesis 6:1-7
It is unclear who the 'sons of God' were who married the 'daughters of men'. A reasonable possibility was the descendants of Seth (the ones who followed God) and the descendants of Cain (the ones who lived their own way). Whatever the case, it is clear that God was unhappy about the mixed marriages.

How does the passage describe humankind? (v5)

How does people's sin make God feel? (v6)

What are the two things God decides to do in response to people's sin? (v3 and 7)

The story of Noah
Read: Genesis 6:8-14
Noah was different from other people. How did Noah find favour with God? (See also Hebrews 11:7)

Did the people of Noah's time deserve punishment?

What was the punishment for their sin?
Read: Genesis 7:22-23

The story of Noah and the flood is a famous one, even to people who don't normally read the Bible.
Read the Noah story in a shortened form. Genesis 7:1-4 and 6-12 and 8:1 and 8:6-12 and 8:15-22.

Based on the above passages, say whether the following statements are 'true' or 'false':
1. It rained for 40 days but not at night.
   True   False

2. Eight people were on the ark.
   True   False

3. God almost forgot about Noah.
   True   False

4. Noah sent out a dove out three times.
   True   False

5. Some people not on the ark survived the flood.
   True   False

6. God decided to always fix the problem of sin with a flood.
   True   False

7. The flood removes sin from the earth forever.
   True   False

Judgment day
God had a plan to save people from sin and did not give up when the world turned evil. He punished sin with a flood but showed mercy by saving Noah and his family. God later provided a permanent solution to our sin by sending Jesus to take the punishment for sin. The day will come when Jesus will return to judge those who reject his solution to sin.

Read: Matthew 24:36-44
What does this passage tell you about the return of Jesus?

How can you be ready for the day that Jesus returns?

If people deserve punishment, and God warns us that the judgment day will come, what should we do for others?

In the beginning ...

Aim (At the end of this study the young people will know the story of Noah, and that God's mercy gives humankind a second chance. They will also understand what a covenant is.

Optional Quick Quiz See page 67.

Share Have everyone share about the promises they have made or have had made to them.

Some instructions for Noah

Ask someone to read Genesis 9:1-7.
Who else was told to populate the earth in Genesis? (Genesis 1:27-28) Adam and Eve. The instructions given to Adam and Eve by God were similar to the ones given to Noah. It is like God is giving people a second chance! A question may arise about whether it is OK to eat blood. Prepare yourself by reading **Leviticus 17:11-12.** The Leviticus passage shows us that God allowed atonement through sacrifice of animals. To 'atone' means to make AT ONE. The atonement is when we are made 'at one' with God and relationship is restored. Jesus has fulfilled the Old Testament law which means that we don't follow the old way anymore. Read also **Romans 3:25** and **Hebrews 9:13-14.**

Why is murder such a serious sin? (v6) Humans are created in the image of God. **Note:** even though sin has ruined relationships, people are still considered to be in the image of God. Give the young people time to tick the boxes to indicate what they believe murder is. Then have them explain their decisions. There are no correct answers yet, this is simply their opinion. The two passages tell us that murder is not only taking a life but also hating someone in our heart. Ask them to review their answers and give them the correct answers: taking a human life, saying something nasty, hating someone. We are supposed to take care of plants and animals but they are not created in the image of God and we are allowed to eat them for food. Killing someone accidentally is not murder, since murder is a deliberate act.

The Covenant

Ask someone to read Genesis 9:8-17. Make sure everyone knows what a covenant is and then take some suggestions. Here are some: marriage, mortgage with a bank, a work/business contract, apprenticeship. 'Covenant' is a term used to describe the relationship between God and humans. The graciousness (undeserved favour) of God for the benefit and blessing of humankind.
What did God promise to humankind and how would he always remind them of his promise?
To never destroy the earth with a flood. He gave the sign of the promise as a rainbow.
Did people remain faithful to God after being rescued from the flood?
(Ask someone to read Genesis 9:20-23.) Noah gets drunk and his son is disrespectful to him.
Examples of God's faithfulness and humankind's unfaithfulness in Genesis 1-9 are:
  • God gave Adam and Eve everything but they wanted more and rebelled. God showed mercy to them and provided clothes, kept them from the tree of life and promised that someone would come and crush the serpent.
  • Although God warned Cain about controlling his anger, Cain killed his brother Abel. God punished Cain but for his security provided a mark of protection on his forehead.
  • God punished sin with a flood but saved Noah and his family.
Share anvy examples where God is faithful even when we are unfaithful. You may want to have one prepared to get started. Read the two passages about God's solution to sin.
  Jeremiah 31:31-34 God made a covenant that sinful people could not break.
  Matthew 26:26-28 Jesus' blood is the permanent solution.

Pray Spend some time in prayer.

In the beginning ...
Noah Part 2: The promise
Genesis 9

Share

What is a promise you have made or that someone has made to you?

Some instructions for Noah

Read: Genesis 9:1-7
Noah and his sons were told to populate the earth (v1 and 7). Who else was told to populate the earth? (Hint: Genesis 1:28).

Why is murder such a serious sin? (v6)

Tick the boxes below to indicate your opinion about what murder is.

❑ Taking a human life.   ❑ Saying something nasty.

❑ Killing someone accidentally.   ❑ Killing an animal.

❑ Hating someone.   ❑ Not watering your pot plants.

Discuss your answers explaining your opinions.

Most people we know have not committed murder. However, look at the following passages:
Matthew 5:21-22

1 John 3:15

What do these verses tell us about murder?

What boxes would you now tick having read these verses?

The Covenant

Read: Genesis 9:8-17
The word covenant simply means 'promise'. It is an agreement between two people or two groups of people binding them to be committed to each other.
Can you think of any examples of a covenant today?

What did God promise to humankind and how would he always remind them of his promise?

Did people remain faithful to God after being rescued from the flood? (See Genesis 9:20-23)

A pattern is emerging that continues through the whole Bible: God is faithful even though people are unfaithful. **What examples have we seen of God's faithfulness and humankind's unfaithfulness in Genesis so far?**

Can you think of some examples today where God is faithful even when we are unfaithful?

How did God keep his promise (covenant) with Noah not to flood the earth again but still deal with sinful people? (See Jeremiah 31:31-34 and Matthew 26:26-28)

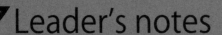

Leader's notes
The Tower of Babel
Genesis 10 and 11

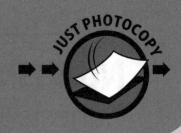

Aim (At the end of this study the young people will know the story of the Tower of Babel and learn that God's plan for people was not ruined by their sin. They will also understand that they need to allow God to control all areas of their own lives.

Optional Quick Quiz See page 67.

Share To introduce the study, check if everyone can say a word in a foreign language and then ask what language they would like to be able to speak.

Table of the nations (Chapter 10)

Read the section about Noah's descendants.
Optional Exercise: Get the young people to engage in an activity that requires co-operation but tell them they are not allowed to speak to each other. For example blindfold everyone, number them and then tell them to get in order without speaking. This is a fun way to introduce the story of the tower of Babel.

The tower of Babel

Ask one or a few people to read: Genesis 11:1-9.
Note: The tower was built in the plains of Shinar which is the Hebrew translation of 'Babylon'. Later in the Bible God's people were sent to Babylon as a punishment for rebelling against him. The city of Babylon became the symbol of the place where people rebelled against God, and the New Testament refers to the world today as 'Babylon' (eg Revelation 18).

Why did the people want to build the tower? They wanted to make a name for themselves and not be scattered.

Why do you think this act was considered disobedience against God? It was an attempt to overthrow God by bringing glory to themselves and refusing to fill the earth and subdue it as God had instructed. The tower was a sign of arrogance and rebellion against God.

Note: 'Nothing would be impossible for them' (11:6) probably means there would be no limit to how sinful they could be.

How did God punish their sin? He confused their language and scattered them.

In what ways do people today try to build their lives without God? Share some answers. You may want to have some already prepared. Some suggestions are: they live their life ignoring God; they try to build successful lives through study or work with no thought of God; they will make decisions that will benefit themselves but not others.

In what areas of your own life do you feel God needs to be more involved? Ask the young people to write a number between 1 and 10 to indicate the level of God's involvement in their decision-making in that area of their life and then discuss their answers. Ask for volunteers to share the area/s in their life that they need to allow God to take control of. **Note:** God needs to control every area of our life, not just part of it.

Ask one or a few people to read Genesis 11:10 and 26-31.
Who is the famous Bible character in this passage? Abram (explain that his name became lengthened to Abraham). Then have someone read **Genesis 12:1-3 What does this teach us about God's faithfulness?** God continues to bless his people.

Pray Read the section about God's plan to rescue mankind. Spend some time sharing what the group has learned through the study of Genesis 1-11, then pray.

In the beginning ...
The Tower of Babel
Genesis 10 and 11

Share

What is one word you know from another language?

If you could speak any language which one would you speak (and why)?

Table of the nations (Chapter 10)

Chapter 10 contains a table of the nations which records the descendants of the sons of Noah.
Japheth: Not much about him (a genealogy only focuses on those of importance to God's plans).
Ham: Some of the descendants of Ham included Cushites, Babylonians, Assyrians, Canaanites and Philistines. All of these people are recorded in the Bible as wicked and became the arch-enemies of God's people, Israel.
Shem: His descendants are recorded in more detail at the end of Chapter 11. They became the chosen people whom God had blessed.
The record of these people is further evidence that there are two types of people: those who follow God and those who don't.

The tower of Babel

Read: Genesis 11:1-9. Why did the people want to build the tower?

Why do you think this act was considered disobedience against God?
(hint Genesis 1:28; 9:1 and 7)

How did God punish their sin?

In what ways do people today try to build their lives without God?

In what areas of your own life do you feel God needs to be more involved?

Write a number between 1 and 10 to indicate the level of God's involvement in your decision-making in that area of your life (1 = God has no say in this, 10 = God is completely in charge of this).
Then discuss your answers.

- [ ] Your plans for your career.
- [ ] Your choice of partner.
- [ ] The way you spend your money.
- [ ] How you use your time.
- [ ] Your friendships.
- [ ] Other? _____

In which area/s of your life listed above do you need to allow God to take control?

Genesis 11 ends with another genealogy focusing on Noah's descendants through Shem.
Read: Genesis 11:10 and 26-31

Who is the famous Bible character in this passage?

Read about what God says to him in the following chapter. Read: Genesis 12:1-3

What does this teach us about God's faithfulness to humankind?

When God created everything he declared that it was good. However, because of sin, humankind has continued to destroy that which was once good. Nevertheless, God's good plan to rescue humankind from their sin has not changed and he continues to show mercy even though we do not deserve it.

Quick Quiz
The mission of Jesus in Acts

STUDY 2 **The New Community**
Who wrote Acts? Luke.
What did the author do for a living? He was a doctor.
Acts is a sequel to which Gospel? The Gospel of Luke.
How do we know that the contents of the Book of Acts are reliable?
Recorded eyewitness accounts.

STUDY 3 **The Conversion of Saul** (later known as Paul)
Who wrote Acts? Luke.
What did the author do for a living? He was a doctor.
Acts is a sequel to which Gospel? The Gospel of Luke.
How do we know that the contents of the Book of Acts are reliable?
Recorded eyewitness accounts.
What are some things that a Christian community does? From Study 2 (Acts 2:42-47).

STUDY 4 **The Gentiles accepted into God's people**
Who wrote Acts? Luke.
What did the author do for a living? He was a doctor.
Acts is a sequel to which Gospel? The Gospel of Luke.
How do we know that the contents of the Book of Acts are reliable?
Recorded eyewitness accounts.
What are some things that a Christian community does? From Study 2 (Acts 2:42-47).
What are some things you know about Paul (Saul)? From Study 3, but if they know other information
about him, let them share it.

STUDY 5 **Paul the Missionary and Preacher**
Who wrote Acts? Luke.
What did the author do for a living? He was a doctor.
Acts is a sequel to which Gospel? The Gospel of Luke.
How do we know that the contents of the Book of Acts are reliable?
Recorded eyewitness accounts.
What are some things that a Christian community does? From Study 2 (Acts 2:42-47).
What is a Gentile? Not a Jew.
What was the problem solved by the Council of Jerusalem in Acts 15? The Jews were in disagreement
about the basis on which a Gentile is made acceptable to God.
What can you remember about the Apostle Paul (Saul)? From Study 3 (Acts 9).

STUDY 6 **Paul the Prisoner Gives his Testimony**
Who wrote Acts? Luke.
What did the author do for a living? He was a doctor.
Acts is a sequel to which Gospel? The Gospel of Luke.
How do we know that the contents of the Book of Acts are reliable?
Recorded eyewitness accounts.
What are some things that a Christian community does? From Study 2 (Acts 2:42-47).
What is a Gentile? Not a Jew.
What was the problem solved by the Council of Jerusalem in Acts 15? The Jews were in disagreement
about the basis on which a Gentile is made acceptable to God.
What can you remember about the Apostle Paul (Saul)? From Study 3 (Acts 9).
What can you remember from Paul's sermon in Athens? (Acts 17:16-34)

Quick Quiz
In the beginning...
Genesis 1–11

STUDY 2 Genesis 3 – **Sin**
What two things describe people as being in God's image? We rule and we relate.
How many times does Genesis give us the creation story? Twice.
What is the focus in chapter 2 and why?
The creation of people. We are special as we are made in God's image.

STUDY 3 Genesis 4 and 5 – **The Spread of Sin**
What two things describe people as being in God's image? We rule and we relate.
How many times does Genesis give us the creation story? Twice.
What is the focus in chapter 2 and why?
The creation of people. We are special as we are made in God's image.
What was the curse on people because of Adam's sin? Death.

STUDY 4 Genesis 6 to 8 – **Noah Part 1: The Flood**
What two things describe people as being in God's image? We rule and we relate.
How many times does Genesis give us the creation story? Twice.
What is the focus in chapter 2 and why?
The creation of people. We are special as we are made in God's image.
What was the curse on people because of Adam's sin? Death.
What are the two types of people in Genesis 3 and 4?
Those who follow God and those who don't.

STUDY 5 Genesis 9 – **Noah Part II: The Promise**
What two things describe people as being in God's image? We rule and we relate.
How many times does Genesis give us the creation story? Twice.
What is the focus in chapter 2 and why?
The creation of people. We are special as we are made in God's image.
What was the curse on people because of Adam's sin? Death.
What are the two types of people in Genesis 3 and 4?
Those who follow God and those who don't.
How is God's anger and mercy shown in Genesis 6-8 and in the NT?
God punishes sin through the flood and saves the faithful (Noah and his family).
God punishes sin through Jesus and saves the faithful (all who trust in Jesus).
What are some facts you can remember about the Noah story?

STUDY 6 Genesis 10 and 11 – **The Tower of Babel**
What two things describe people as being in God's image? We rule and we relate.
How many times does Genesis give us the creation story? Twice.
What is the focus in chapter 2 and why?
The creation of people. We are special as we are made in God's image.
What was the curse on people because of Adam's sin? Death.
What are the two types of people in Genesis 3 and 4?
Those who follow God and those who don't.
How is God's anger and mercy shown in Genesis 6-8 and in the NT?
God punishes sin through the flood and saves the faithful (Noah and his family).
God punishes sin through Jesus and saves the faithful (all who trust in Jesus).
What are some facts you can remember about the Noah story?
What does the word covenant mean? Promise.

Notes

Notes

Notes

Notes

Notes

Notes

Notes